P9-BVG-781

The Changing Nature of the Academic Deanship

Mimi Wolverton, Walter H. Gmelch,
Joni Montez, Charles T. Nies

ASHE-ERIC Higher Education Report Volume 28, Number 1
Adrianna J. Kezar, Series Editor

Prepared and published by

 **JOSSEY-BASS**
A Wiley Company
San Francisco

In cooperation with

ERIC Clearinghouse on Higher Education
The George Washington University
URL: www.eriche.org

Association for the Study
of Higher Education
URL: http://www.tiger.coe.missouri.edu/~ashe

Graduate School of Education and Human Development
The George Washington University
URL: www.gwu.edu

LIBRARY
COLBY-SAWYER COLLEGE
NEW LONDON, NH 03257

LC
5215
.C35
2001
c.1

#4676291O

The Changing Nature of the Academic Deanship
Mimi Wolverton, Walter H. Gmelch, Joni Montez, and Charles T. Nies
ASHE-ERIC Higher Education Report Volume 28, Number 1
Adrianna J. Kezar, Series Editor

This publication was prepared partially with funding from the Office of
Educational Research and Improvement, U.S. Department of Education, under
contract no. ED-99-00-0036. The opinions expressed in this report do not
necessarily reflect the positions or policies of OERI or the Department.

Copyright © 2001 Jossey-Bass, A Publishing Unit of John Wiley & Sons, Inc. All
rights reserved. Reproduction or translation of any part of this work beyond that
permitted by Sections 107 or 108 of the 1976 United States Copyright Act without
permission of the copyright owner is unlawful. Requests for permission or further
information should be addressed to the Permissions Department, John Wiley &
Sons, Inc., 605 Third Avenue, New York, NY 10158-0012; (212) 850-6011,
fax (212) 850-6008, e-mail: permreq@wiley.com.

ISSN 0884-0040   ISBN 0-7879-5835-2

The ASHE-ERIC Higher Education Report is part of the Jossey-Bass Higher
and Adult Education Series and is published six times a year by Jossey-Bass,
350 Sansome Street, San Francisco, California 94104-1342.

For subscription information, see the Back Issue/Subscription Order Form in the
back of this journal.

Prospective authors are strongly encouraged to contact Adrianna Kezar, Director,
ERIC Clearinghouse on Higher Education, at (202) 296-2597 ext. 14 or
akezar@eric-he-edu.

Visit the Jossey-Bass Web site at **www.josseybass.com.**

Printed in the United States of America on acid-free recycled paper
containing 100 percent recovered waste paper, of which at least 20 percent is
postconsumer waste.

Executive Summary

The leadership linchpin that holds an organization together lies midway between those perceived as leaders and those upon whose work the reputation of the organization rests. In universities today, academic deans fill this role. This monograph provides a compilation of scholarly literature written about academic deans. The premise upon which it builds suggests that changes external to the academy have affected the nature of the academic deanship and will continue to do so into the foreseeable future. With this in mind, the authors seek to answer four questions about academic deans: Who are they and what do they do? What challenges do they face? What strategies might they use to meet these challenges? What can universities do to help deans become more effective?

Who Are They and What Do They Do?

While the deanship's lineage can be traced back to medieval universities, its emergence in U.S. universities is a relatively recent phenomenon (Dibden, 1968). It was not until 1913 that the position gained universal acceptance (Deferrari, 1956). The profile of deans over time has changed slightly but still remains predominantly white and male. Deans continue to be about the same age, in their midfifties. They are married and have been in their positions five to six years on average.

Strong scholarly credentials distinguish most deans. Early on, presidents selected deans directly from faculty ranks. Today, the majority are selected by a committee of faculty and administrators. More than 60 percent have been department chairs, with the clearest career trajectories manifesting themselves in colleges of liberal arts at research universities. Their duties have moved, over time, from being almost exclusively student focused to include a multifaceted array of roles, such as budgeting and fundraising, personnel and work environment management, program oversight, and external public relations. As a result, deans experience increasing ambiguity and conflict, which raise their levels of work-related stress.

What Challenges Do They Face?

Deans come to the position, for the most part, underprepared to deal with strained fiscal resources, externally imposed accountability pressures, demand for relevant curricula and programs, technology advancement and educational delivery, faculty ill equipped to meet student and system demands, diversity, and professional and personal imbalance. They receive the charge to lead change in the face of shifting demographics of students, changing political and economic attitudes, demands placed on them by the corporate sector, and rapid advancements in technology.

Currently, greater numbers of students who are more diverse than ever before attend college. These students expect faculty to engage them in learning activities that incorporate technology and relate to the workplace. And they expect to have mentors in the faculty and administration who look like them and will be committed to supporting their educational efforts. At the same time, competing social problems, such as crime, racial inequality, and health and welfare, make it difficult for institutions of higher education to secure a significant portion of available public funds. And, increasingly, the corporate sector has signaled its disillusionment with the quality of preparation members of the workforce receive at colleges. Simultaneously, businesses engage in research partnerships where patenting and dissemination restrictions could limit academic freedom. Finally, technological advancements that change daily create a constant need for higher education to keep current.

These advancements help drive curricular reform in terms of both content and delivery.

What Strategies Can They Use to Meet These Challenges?

Universities expect deans to lead their colleges. To do so, deans must ensure that their colleges realize university missions in terms of instruction and research. The authors offer an overall strategy—one that moves deans as managers of day-to-day operations to deans as leaders in a dynamic environment. In addition, they offer six specific strategies that relate to persistent challenges: create a diverse culture, know the legal environment, become technologically connected, strategically manage and secure financial resources, seek and maintain professional and personal balance, and nurture the integrity of your college. Diversity strategies focus on the assessment of college history, policies and procedures, the college's psychological climate, and the behaviors of people within it. Strategies that relate to legal issues deal with laws that pertain to discriminatory student admissions and faculty hiring, tenure, and promotion practices; academic freedom; and students' expectations for program quality. A final section suggests how deans might go about instilling a culture of ethical practice within their colleges. Technology strategies seek solutions to issues of student learning and education delivery, personnel productivity, and the use of fiscal resources. Funding strategies address two areas—fiscal management and resource procurement. Balance strategies help deans strike a balance between their professional and personal lives, scholarship and leadership, and long-term agendas and short-term tasks. These strategies help deans take control of their agendas through time, boundary, and stress management. College integrity has to do with how the general public perceives its colleges and universities. It hinges on the success universities have in building alliances with people and organizations in a fashion that fulfills recognizable public needs. Deans can take several approaches to this endeavor—redefining faculty work, reframing academic departments, refocusing department chairs, reconnecting colleges with communities, and revisiting the concept of change leadership.

What Can Universities Do to Help Deans Become More Effective?

Universities provide the broader context within which deans succeed or fail. As such, universities have a role to play in ensuring that their deans lead well. The final section provides ideas that can help universities further the leadership abilities of their deans. Its components include selection, socialization, development, and evaluation. A final topic, rethinking the position, piques the imagination.

Contents

Foreword

The academic dean has been called the cornerstone of higher education, providing an important foundation to institutions, and creating policies and encouraging practices that improve and sustain. At a time when higher education is facing tremendous challenges from technological advances, diversity, new competition, and cost containment, deans, as the foundation of universities, will be looked on to provide needed leadership and direction.

It is this realization that led coauthors Mimi Wolverton, Walter Gmelch, Joni Montez, and Charles Nies to develop this monograph on the changing nature of the academic deanship. One of the best selling monographs in the ASHE-ERIC Series, *The Department Chair: New Roles, Responsibilities, and Challenges,* explores the ways department chairs shape and frame the institution and highlights the challenges they face. This monograph provides similar key information by answering four questions: Who are deans and what do they do? What challenges do they face? What strategies can they use to meet these challenges? And what can universities do to help deans become more effective? The answers to these questions are based on a long-term study of deans conducted by the authors, which provides current data for the answers. The authors focus on several themes that deans noted are challenges in today's environment: fiscal constraints and accountability, demands for curricular relevance, legal issues, funding, technical advancements and educational delivery systems, shifting demographics, faculty-student-system incongruence, and balance.

The authors begin by examining the evolution of the role of dean from medieval times, examining issues such as career path, selection, function, role conflict, the need for increasingly specialized knowledge, and growing expectations. A thorough review of the dean's current role finds it characterized by ambiguity, stress, and conflict. Moreover, preparation is minimal, especially for new challenges resulting from political and economic changes, demands of corporitization, and technological advances. The dean's role is also marked by increasing professionalism; deans must understand legal issues, fundraising, pedagogical innovation, and finance. And most deans are not socialized to their role and have no mentoring, as the person who previously held the position is usually gone. It is no wonder that it is difficult for deans to execute their role as leaders and facilitators of change. This monograph highlights the need for universities to provide formal preparation and ongoing evaluation so that deans are able to flourish in these difficult positions.

Several other ASHE-ERIC monographs address similar topics and complement and enhance *The Changing Nature of the Academic Deanship. The Costs and Uses of Faculty Compensation; Managing Costs in Higher Education;* and *Fund Raising in Higher Education* address financial issues. *The Academic Administrator and the Law* and *Due Process and Higher Education* provide key information on pertinent legal issues. Performance and hiring issues are reviewed in *Posttenure Faculty Development; Faculty Recruitment, Retention, and Fair Employment;* and *Diversity in Higher Education: Women and Minority Faculty in the Academic Workplace.* Three monographs examine how administrators create change: *Academic Departments: How They Work and How They Change; Instituting Enduring Innovations;* and *Creating Distinctiveness.* Last, a major theme in this monograph is personal and institutional integrity: *Values and Ethics* in Higher Education addresses these issues.

A wealth of information is available for deans, helping to enhance day-to-day problem solving and providing answers to crises.

Adrianna Kezar
Series Editor
Director, ERIC Clearinghouse on Higher Education
Assistant Professor, George Washington University

Introduction and Purpose

LEADERSHIP IS THE LINCHPIN that holds an organization together while at the same time moving it forward. Its focus lies midway between those perceived by the public as leaders and those upon whose work the reputation of the organization rests. In universities today, academic deans fill this role (A. E. Austin, 1984; M. J. Austin, Ahearn, and English, 1997b; Fagin, 1997; Thiessen and Howey, 1998).

Driven by academic discipline from below and constrained by budgetary concerns from above, college deans straddle a jittery enterprise whose members at once cling to tradition and toy with the notion of breaking out of the mold. A desire for normalcy pushes faculty to find deans steeped in disciplinary ritual; the necessity of dealing with fiscal constraints, competition for students, demands for accountability, the ramifications of changing technology, and the shifting demographics of the country drives an administrative expectation that these deans be change agents bent on improving the institution (Allen-Meares, 1997; Wisniewski, 1998).

In essence, deans serve two masters. And therein lies the irony. On the one hand, university presidents and provosts advocate, and sometimes demand, responses to the external environment that require innovation and creativity that only faculty can provide. On the other, faculty,

> Driven by academic discipline from below and constrained by budgetary concerns from above, college deans straddle a jittery enterprise whose members at once cling to tradition and toy with the notion of breaking out of the mold.

loyal to academic disciplines but not necessarily to the universities for which they work, are not interested in expending time and energy on issues they deem someone else's concern (M. Wolverton, Gmelch, and Sorenson, 1998; Yarger, 1998). Indeed, faculty pursue professional goals to which they are committed, such as research and teaching, and resist any that are externally imposed (Arends, 1998).

Paradoxically, deans continually build a case for two primary college endeavors—research and teaching—but no longer participate to any great extent in either (M. J. Austin, Ahearn, and English, 1997b). This situation led one cynic to claim, "A dean is not intelligent enough to be a professor and too intelligent to be a president (Cleveland, 1968, p. 232). Another suggested that "the qualified academic administrator is the professor who answers his mail" (Rosenheim, 1963, p. 226). Such perspectives perpetuate a view of deans as paper shufflers charged by their faculty with manipulating the system in their favor (Dibden, 1968; Stein and Trachtenberg, 1993). Any dean bent on changing the system encounters a healthy distrust among faculty.

These views also shortchange deans and understate the complexities they face. Barzun (1945, p. 76) called deans "overworked, harassed arbitrators, housekeepers, orators, and employers." In a sense, it may not have as much to do with responding to correspondence as it does with "know[ing] which mail to ignore" (Gould, 1964, p. 71). Today's dynamic educational environment serves up challenges that early deans never encountered. For decades, deans functioned in an environment that remained stable. Change, over time, was slow, gradual, and incremental. Deans had the luxury of doing what they had always done or of having to adjust only slightly. In contrast, during the latter half of the twentieth century, shifts in the external environment became more rapid, more violent, more radical. As such, the inability of deans to respond to change or, better yet, anticipate it can threaten the viability of their colleges.

The title "dean" appears to be a desirous one because during its short history we have seen a proliferation of positions and people who carry that name: academic deans, deans of students, men, women, freshmen, faculty, instruction, studies, graduate schools, and administration and student affairs. Some of these positions can clearly be associated with types of responsibilities (deans of students and deans of graduate schools, for example) and others with institutional type. Deans of instruction, for instance, are often found in community and technical colleges. Increasingly, the term "academic dean" has been reserved for those institutional leaders who head discipline-specific colleges within universities. It is this latter group of deans on which the authors of this monograph concentrate.

Even after the focus is limited to academic deans, the picture remains fragmented and murky. Much of what has been written about academic deans draws from personal experience and is anecdotal in nature (M. J. Austin, Ahearn, and English, 1997b; Fagin, 1997; Fenstermacher, 1995; Morris, 1981; Rosovsky, 1990). Some researchers prescribe what deans ought to do (Arends, 1998; Creswell and England, 1994; Thiessen and Howey, 1998; Townsend and Bassoppo-Moyo, 1996; Tucker and Bryan, 1988). Many demographic and analytic accounts are dated and narrowly focused. For instance, Gould (1964) wrote about liberal arts deans and Dupont in Dibden (1968) provided a historical overview of the liberal arts dean; Griffiths and McCarty (1980) and Andersen and King (1987) studied deans of education colleges; Abramson and Moss (1977) described the backgrounds of law deans and Bowker (1982a) of deans of sociology; P. M. Miller (1989) sought to understand business deans; and Otis and Caragonne (1979) surveyed former deans of schools of social work to determine why they had resigned. Others studied midlevel academic leadership but failed to analyze deans separately or ignored them altogether. Robbins, Schmitt, Ehinger, and Welliver's (1994) study of deans and chairs in colleges of education provides an example of the first type of research, and R. A. Scott's (1978) examination of administrators exemplifies the second.

Four questions about deans drive the organization of this monograph: Who are they and what do they do? What challenges do they face? What strategies might they use to meet these challenges? And what can universities do to help deans become more effective? The first section of this monograph provides readers with a better understanding of the evolution of the deanship as a position and of the people who pursue it. To do so, it presents a series of snapshots over time of the people who have been, or currently are, academic deans.

Who Are Deans
and What Do They Do?

Who Are They?

While the deanship's lineage can be traced back to medieval universities, its emergence in U.S. universities is a relatively recent phenomenon (Dibden, 1968). The first dean, appointed in 1816, oversaw the medical school at Harvard (McGrath, 1936, 1999). His primary charge: to be friendly and charitable to students (Brubacher and Rudy, 1958). Between 1830 and 1870, Harvard and other universities added deans in the fields of law, divinity, and liberal arts and sciences; by 1913, the position had gained universal acceptance (Deferrari, 1956; McGinnis, 1933). Traditionally, colleges elevated their most senior faculty members to the deanship. Before 1950, those eligible to fill these slots were white males who, to be considered for the position, were older, well-established scholars (M. J. Austin, Ahearn, and English, 1997b). This pattern shifted somewhat after World War II, particularly after the civil rights movement in the 1960s, when academic leadership positions began to open up to women and people of color.

In an attempt to gain some idea of the persons who filled the deanship during this period of time, we made the assumption that demographic portraits of deans, regardless of academic discipline, bore more similarities than differences.[1] Four studies conducted by Gould (reporting 1961 data), Griffiths and McCarty (1978 data), Moore (1979 data), and Miller (late 1980s data) give fuller profiles than most.[2] A fifth study, conducted ten years or more after these first studies, updates and further broadens the profile (Gmelch, Wolverton, Wolverton, and Sarros, 1999; M. Wolverton, Gmelch, and Wolverton, 2000; M. Wolverton, Wolverton, and Gmelch, 1999).[3]

Deans a Generation Ago

One of the earliest comprehensive pictures of deans examined liberal arts colleges (Gould, 1964). These all-male deans worked in colleges at public and private institutions. Their colleges varied in size from fewer than 500 students and 30 faculty to more than 20,000 students and 900 faculty. Even so, no discernible differences in responses existed across deans. On average, they were fifty-six years old, and most had been in their positions for six years. More than 70 percent claimed that evaluation of faculty in their colleges was, at best, informal; fewer than one-third used standardized department chair rating forms, and about 40 percent used student evaluations. Sixty percent of them taught at least one class per year. Those who did not teach typically cited having too heavy an administrative work load to spare the time for teaching. Forty-five percent of them continued to engage in research; 30 percent published, but more than one-half of them had shifted their research interests to focus on the issues they confronted as deans. The majority of respondents in this study did attempt to stay current in their disciplines through reading (Gould, 1964).

These deans did not view themselves as leaders but as catalysts of faculty opinion and decision making. They had no inclination to shape opinion or set direction. If what they deemed essential for the college did not conform to faculty sentiment, they abandoned the idea. The greatest need that liberal arts deans in this time period identified was more time. The majority believed that ever-increasing administrative duties were driving scholarly people out of the deanship (Gould, 1964).

Ten years later, the presence of women and minorities in the deanship began to be reflected in study findings. Sixteen percent of education deans in Griffiths and McCarty's (1980) sample were females, although none held positions at doctorate-granting universities. In 1981, Moore (1982) examined more than 650 deans who headed colleges in 29 different academic areas. She found a similar participation pattern in that about 14 percent of the sample were women. More than one-half of these women were housed in schools or colleges of nursing, home economics, arts and sciences, and continuing education. Women also tended to be located at baccalaureate institutions. No women in the sample were deans of business, engineering, law, medicine, or physical education. Law deans also exhibited a skewed gender profile during this period (eighty-two males, two females in the Abramson and Moss [1977] study). These last statistics suggest that colleges of academic disciplines, such as law, engineering, architecture, medicine, veterinary medicine, and business, traditionally housed only at research universities, were almost totally led by male deans at this time (Van Alstyne and Withers, 1977).

Deans were predominantly white. At most, about 6 percent carried minority status; most of them were black, and the majority of them headed colleges of education (Abramson and Moss, 1977, Griffiths and McCarty, 1980; Moore, 1982). Here again the assumption can be made that ethnic and racial participation in many disciplines was essentially nonexistent in the 1960s and 1970s. Ten years later, Andersen and King (1987) found a similar profile in education deans: most were white males, although the percentage of minority deans had doubled to 12 percent and the percentage of female deans in their sample had risen to 33 percent.

The majority of education, sociology, and law deans during this period were fifty years or older. Most had been in their positions for five to six years, with the notable exception of law deans, who seemed to average less than four years. Close to 90 percent of male deans were married, but less than one-half of the female deans had spouses (Bowker, 1982a; Griffiths and McCarty, 1980; Moore, 1982). Most education deans no longer worked in the classroom on a regular basis.

Deans felt that they were less productive in the area of personal scholarship since entering the deanship. Less than one-half of them said they engaged in any research whatsoever. Those who had continued to pursue personal research agendas spent less time on it than they did before taking the deanship. Overwhelmingly, deans believed that the deanship restricted them from pursuing personal and professional activities. And they found work-related stress problematic and tied to a perceived lack of preparation (Griffiths and McCarty, 1980).

Current Deans

The most current demographic data on deans come from the National Study of Academic Deans (NSAD) conducted in the late 1990s (Gmelch, Wolverton,

Wolverton, and Sarros, 1999; M. Wolverton, Wolverton, and Gmelch, 1999; M. Wolverton, Gmelch, and Wolverton, 2000) and several studies that examined the length of time spent in the deanship (Johns, 1986; P. M. Miller, 1989; O'Reilly, 1994; Robbins, Schmitt, Ehinger, and Welliver, 1994). The NSAD was structured to generate a large proportion of women in the sample; as a result, female deans were well represented, with 41 percent of the sample, and almost one-half of them worked in colleges of nursing. A slightly higher percentage of male (60 percent) than female (50 percent) deans worked in public universities. Of the male respondents, 32 percent of the sample were employed at research, 48 percent at comprehensive, and 20 percent at baccalaureate universities. There is some indication in the literature that women are typically more successful in smaller private schools than in research universities (Ost and Twale, 1989; Touchton and Davis, 1991; Van Alstyne and Withers, 1977); however, the NSAD shows somewhat different patterns. Thirty-six percent of the female deans in this study worked at research, 43 percent at comprehensive, and 21 percent at baccalaureate universities.

Women do seem to be securing deanships in areas such as nursing, education, and liberal arts, but not in all fields, and especially not in mathematics, science, and business (Bronstein, Rothblum, and Solomon, 1993; Catsambio, 1994; Touchton and Davis, 1991). A comparison of business deans across time suggests that the percentage of female deans remained stable at 4 percent from 1988 to 1997 (P. M. Miller, 1989; M. Wolverton, Wolverton, and Gmelch, 1999). In contrast, males remain underrepresented in deanships in historically feminized disciplines, such as nursing (in the NSAD, 7 percent of nursing deans were men).

Roughly 12 percent of the participants in the NSAD carried minority status (10 percent of the men, 14 percent of the women); slightly more than one-half of these respondents were African American. The majority (57 percent) of them worked at public institutions. Thirty-two percent were employed at research universities, 41 percent at comprehensive, and 27 percent at baccalaureate institutions. The largest proportion (35 percent) headed colleges of education, followed by liberal arts (31 percent). Fewer deans of minority status in this study were found in nursing (20 percent) or business (13 percent) colleges.

Deans were typically between fifty-three and fifty-four years old; more than 90 percent of the men but fewer than 60 percent of the women were married. The average tenure as dean for women was five years and for men, six (P. M. Miller, 1989; M. Wolverton, Wolverton, and Gmelch, 1999). Other studies that examined the length of time spent in the deanship found that deans served much shorter terms. For deans of education, the mean time in the position was four and one-half years (Robbins, Schmitt, Ehinger, and Welliver, 1994), and for law and business school deans, three and one-half years (Johns, 1986; O'Reilly, 1994). While all deans suggested that they had difficulty balancing work and their private lives and in pursuing their scholarly endeavors, women expressed higher levels of work-related stress and lower levels of satisfaction with personal scholarship since taking the deanship than did men (M. Wolverton, Wolverton, and Gmelch, 1999).

Over a forty-year period, we have seen an influx of women and minorities into the deanship, but they remain underrepresented, especially in professional schools other than nursing and education.

In sum, over a forty-year period, we have seen an influx of women and minorities into the deanship, but they remain underrepresented, especially in professional schools other than nursing and education. Interestingly, female deans are still significantly less likely to be married when compared with male deans. This finding may indicate that after more than twenty years, the job and societal norms in general remain such that women in leadership positions find themselves unable to pursue both marriage and a career. Distribution across institutional type changed somewhat since 1980, with more women and minority deans located in research universities. Tenure in the position did not seem to change substantially, although some research suggests otherwise, and all deans still find it difficult to balance their personal and professional lives and to engage in scholarly endeavors.

Career Paths of Deans Over Time

In the eyes of many faculty, deans are unnecessary, occupational nuisances (M. J. Austin, Ahearn, and English, 1997b). Such a view precludes most from entering their careers as faculty with the notion of one day becoming a dean. On the basis of his reflections on education deans, Morris (1981) suggested that one of four paths leads to the deanship. The first he calls *professional ascension*. Those faculty taking this route move from full professor to department chair (and/or associate dean) to dean (Socolow, 1978). An alternative path, the *trained administrator,* moves prospective deans from the line position of assistant dean to dean. A third possibility brings outside leadership into the college, perhaps a former business executive or military officer. Morris refers to this scenario as the *managerial outside transfer.* Finally, he poses the *political appointment,* or knowing the right people and being in the right place at the right time, as a viable track to the deanship.

In early studies, about two-thirds of liberal arts deans had been department chairs, but most had no prior experience in the dean's office. None of them came from outside the academy (Gould, 1964), and education deans (82 percent) tended to have had well established academic careers. Almost 60 percent were hired as deans within their own colleges. But beyond that, commonalities ceased to exist. Fewer than one-third of them had held any prior administrative position, only 12 percent had been department chairs, another 12 percent had been associate deans, and only 3 percent had been both. Almost no one (less than 1 percent) had been a dean before taking his/her current position (Griffiths and McCarty, 1980), in contrast to deans of law schools, about 15 percent of whom had served in prior deanships (Abramson and Moss, 1977). In Moore's fairly comprehensive work, 29 percent of deans had been department chairs before becoming deans, 16 percent had been associate deans, 10 percent came from outside the academy; and 6 percent had been both department chairs and associate deans during their academic careers. More than one-half of the deans in her study had no prior administrative experience.

By the late 1980s and 1990s, deans still did not follow a set career trajectory, although the route to the deanship does show some signs of change. Today, more than 60 percent of deans across the four disciplines studied had been chairs. And while women were significantly less likely than their male counterparts to have been chairs, a great many of them had filled this position sometime before taking the deanship. Minority-status deans (64 percent) had also been chairs. Such findings seem to indicate that the department chair's position may be a jumping-off point for the deanship, especially at research universities. In addition, 38 percent of female deans had been associate deans, and a fair number of deans had experience as directors or coordinators, suggesting that these positions are at least as viable training grounds as the department chair position appears to be. A growing number of deans seem to be gaining management experience outside the academy before coming to the deanship as well. These trends may all signify a recognition on the part of universities and deans alike that some form of training is crucial. They may also be a reflection of how deans are selected. This consideration seems to be important, given the potential significance of the position (P. M. Miller, 1989; M. Wolverton and Gonzales, 2000).

The Selection of Deans Over Time

Early on, presidents appointed deans with little or no input from faculty (Griffiths and McCarty, 1980), a pattern that seems to have held true into the 1960s, when Gould (1964) reported that two-thirds of the deans in his study had been selected by presidents or presidents in consultation with boards. Since that time, faculty have worked diligently to increase their voices in the selection process and to limit those of central administrators. The result seems to be a heavy emphasis on the qualities that make deans respected scholars but not necessarily good administrators (Bower, 1993; Twale, 1997).

In general, job descriptions of deanships derive from memories of previous successes and failures and are not necessarily designed with any clear understanding of what someone in the position will be required to do or what skills and aptitudes he/she will need to possess to carry out the charge (Birnbaum, 1990, 1992; Cahn, 1997; Crawford, 1983; Lutz, 1979; Twombly, 1992). In fact, in the late 1970s, a posting for a dean of liberal arts at an Ivy League institution read, "Administrative experience is not a prerequisite for the position" (R. A. Scott, 1978, p. 3). To complicate matters further, colleges may advertise for a candidate already identified or groomed for the position (Rachels, 1993; Tracy, 1986). Consistently, no matter which decade, it appears that one-half of all deans are already faculty members in the colleges of which they become dean (Griffiths and McCarty, 1980; M. Wolverton, Wolverton, and Gmelch, 1999).

In a review of advertisements for dean positions, researchers found the following criteria listed in order of preference: earned doctorate, demonstrated capacity as a teacher and scholar, commitment to particular values, and evidence of administrative ability (this last criterion was listed in less than one-half of the job descriptions) (Griffiths and McCarty, 1980; Reid and Rogers, 1981; Twombly, 1992). In part, the character of a previous dean also helped determine the requirements for future deans. For instance, if the previous dean had an excellent reputation as a scholar and if this reputation were mirrored by current faculty, then other characteristics, such as a need for strong inter-personal skills or an ability to raise funds, might be emphasized (Twombly, 1992). Similarly, Twale (1997) examined *Chronicle of Higher Education* adver-tisements in 1993 and 1994 and found a comparable list of requirements to those cited earlier. Administrative experience was mentioned more often than research and scholarship, however, and administrative experience outside higher education was a frequently added prerequisite. One final criterion, missing in most of these accounts but present in deans' accounts of what helps sustain them in the position, is a healthy sense of humor (Blum, 1994; Grossman, 1981; Yingling, 1981). Humor provides perspective.

We now have a picture of who deans are, but to better understand them, we must grasp what it is that deans do. The next section of this monograph details historical perceptions of the roles of academic deans. In particular, it builds an empirically based view of the roles of these deans in the last half of the twentieth century.

What Do They Do?

Despite the position's almost 200-year existence, the role of academic dean has never been standardized (Hawkes, 1930). Indeed, defining the deanship has always been an elusive task because it lacks uniformity in content and function (Dupont, 1968). At one time or another, deans in U.S. colleges have been expected to be "all things to all people." Faculty leader, scholar, student adviser and disciplinarian, admissions officer, bookkeeper, personnel manager, fundraiser—deans have done it all (Thiessen and Howey, 1998; Tucker and Bryan, 1988).

At its inception and into the 1930s, the deanship focused on student concerns (Hawkes, 1930). Of the twenty most frequently assigned functions during this period, twelve dealt with student issues, such as discipline, recruitment, advising, excusing class absences, and freshman orientation. In addition, deans served as registrars and admissions officers for their colleges and sometimes housed and fed students as well (Deferrari, 1956; Dibden, 1968; Dupont, 1968; R. A. Scott, 1979). Six of the remaining duties commonly listed focused on curricular supervision, improvement of instruction, and faculty evaluation. Only two administrative tasks, giving general advice on college policies and reporting annually on the academic health of the college, seemed important to these early deans (Higgins, 1946; Milner, 1936; Ward, 1934).

Since 1890, however, with the emergence of the registrar's office, deans' responsibilities steadily moved away from a student perspective (Hawkes, 1930). In one of the earliest studies of deans, McGrath (1936) examined the roles of academic deans at thirty-two U.S. institutions between 1860 and 1933. Most (97 percent) of the sample had teaching assignments. Few gave any "indication that the job was becoming a purely administrative one" (McGrath, 1936, p. 605). None mentioned student affairs–type concerns, suggesting that the role was either assumed or on the decline. These men continued to engage in research as true scholar-deans (M. J. Austin, Ahearn, and English, 1997b). Indeed, deans during this era sought to maintain their faculty identities while engaging in some administrative responsibilities on the side (R. A. Scott, 1979).

By the mid-1940s, deans actively supervised curricula, faculty, and budgets, with less of their time devoted to direct interaction with students (Forrest, 1951; McGrath, 1947; Woodburne, 1950). As Gould's deans approached the 1960s, they dealt almost exclusively with these first issues, especially if they were located at larger institutions (Corson, 1960). The final devolution of student-based responsibilities came with the creation of the dean of student affairs position in the early 1960s (Dibden, 1968).

These shifts in responsibility in part were the result of the changing nature of college presidencies during this period. With the large influx of students after World War II and the introduction of the Government Services

Readjustment Act of 1944, and promoted by the civil rights movement in the 1960s, college and university presidents faced expansion problems and levels of public scrutiny never before experienced. These pressures required them to turn their attention to fundraising and public relations. In doing so, they relinquished more of their duties to deans (Tucker and Bryan, 1988). Two concerns of deans during this time—dealing with extraordinary circumstances, such as student protests, and curriculum and program development—suggested a broadening of the responsibilities associated with the position (R. A. Scott, 1979). Presidents in effect became external officers and deans internal ones. In the 1960s, deans indicated that dealing with faculty relations and morale consumed the greatest amount of their time and required the greatest skill, followed by faculty recruitment, curricular work, and budgets. Serving on committees and performing routine administrative tasks, such as correspondence and report writing, took time but little skill (Gould, 1964).

With the addition of budget responsibilities and faculty promotion and selection, the status of deans grew (Corson, 1960). Indeed, as their primary functions changed, deans of larger colleges began to resemble presidents of small colleges (Gould, 1964). In a "very real sense, academic dean[s] of large colleges [became] businessmen" (Ginzberg, 1959, p. 150). As such, they found themselves justifying budgets and searching for efficiencies and economies of scale. Increasingly, they spent more time reporting to foundations and government bodies, participating in extracurricular activities out of a sense of obligation, and dealing with sponsored research issues, including those that arose from the unevenness of this type of funding across disciplines (Gould, 1964). Ultimately, as coordination became a greater issue, universities inserted an administrative layer, the office of the provost, between presidents and deans to relieve some of the pressure experienced at both administrative levels (Stein and Trachtenberg, 1993).

During the 1970s and 1980s, external budget constraints on universities moved them operationally toward the ranks of big business. The dean became the "critical fulcrum" between faculty and students, on one hand, and the larger organization, on the other. At stake for the former groups were academic and institutional integrity. At stake for the latter group was economic viability (Morris, 1981). R. I. Miller (1974) contended that when the expansion of higher education slowed in the 1970s, deans focused on the inner workings of their colleges to run more cost-effective operations. They engaged in academic performance evaluation to determine whether faculty were functioning effectively and in faculty development efforts to improve efficiency.

Over the past thirty to forty years, as universities grew in size and complexity, the deanship became decidedly more managerial in nature.

In addition to these roles, deans faced undertakings, such as grievance mediation and due process proceedings associated with contract termination, that forced them to take on quasi-legal duties. As student traumas, racial tensions, and fiscal crises increased, deans moved into the arena of crisis management. Finally, Miller mentions that deans during this period had a key role to play as change agents (Dill, 1980; Feltner and Goodsell, 1972; R. I. Miller, 1974).

Although some deans identified organizing responsibilities, staff development, liaison and public relations functions, program development, and budget-related activities as major functions of the deanship, most did not (Cyphert and Zimpher, 1980). Nursing deans during this period appeared more cognizant of the primacy of budgeting, evaluation, planning, and leadership (Drennan, 1983; Grossman, 1981; Hawken, 1981).

Over the past thirty to forty years, as universities grew in size and complexity, the deanship became decidedly more managerial in nature. Presidents began shifting external duties, such as alumni relations and fundraising, in part to deans. Academic deans, although still charged with the intellectual leadership of their colleges, were also expected to be fiscal experts, fundraisers, politicians, and diplomats (Dibden, 1968; Gould, 1964; Mintzberg, 1973; Tucker and Bryan, 1988). As a result, many college heads became scholar-deans in name only (Gould, 1964).

Role Expectations Today

Such pressures helped solidify the academic dean's role. Whether at a Research I university or a small private college, the dean's primary task evolved into the maintenance of balance between the various external and internal demands placed on the institution. Deans today are responsible for personnel, budgetary, policy, governance, development and fundraising, and other oversight functions (Tucker and Bryan, 1988). As such, they are expected to take on administrative identities commonly associated with corporate business managers: figurehead, leader, liaison, monitor, disseminator, spokesperson, entrepreneur, disturbance handler, resource allocator, and negotiator (P. M. Miller, 1989; Mintzberg, 1973).

Because of their powerful and ubiquitous presence in universities, academic deans regularly interface with presidents, faculty, curricula, and external entities, each influencing and benefiting from the college in specific ways (Twombly, 1992). Deans answer to the faculty, students, staff, central administration, corporate sponsors, alumni groups, and outside funding agencies and must conscientiously serve all of these masters if they are to succeed in the role (P. M. Miller, 1989; Wisniewski, 1998). In essence, deans must "go up, down, across, and out" to ensure success for their colleges (Fagin, 1997, p. 97). Effective deans use adaptive and instinctive strategies—"that funny feeling in the pit of the stomach"—to accommodate the expanded demands of the position (Yarger, 1998, p. 141). They must exhibit leadership traits such as vision, integrity, and perceptiveness and possess the ability to encourage communication and compromise as they work on behalf of the faculty and the college (Wisniewski, 1998).

Currently, deans foster good teaching, represent their colleges, engage in financial planning and budgeting, build and maintain good work environments within their colleges, provide direction, and recruit strong faculty (W. E. Gardner, 1992; Gmelch, Wolverton, Wolverton, and Sarros, 1999). The teaching imperative addresses the liaison role between central administration and the faculty; it includes building relationships and communicating effectively the needs of faculty, staff, and students to garner support for new academic initiatives and support a work environment conducive to scholarship. Representing the college reflects the need to communicate to senior administration what is occurring within the college, using both quantitative and qualitative data to tell the story (Castenell and Tarule, 1997). The financial aspects of the position have expanded beyond overseeing budgets to include securing new funds, particularly from alumni and "friends" of the institution (Mercer, 1997; P. M. Miller, 1989). Zimpher (1995) notes that some deans spend as much as 50 percent of their time on external fundraising activities. Providing direction refers to setting long-range college goals, communicating the college's mission to employees and constituents, and being responsible for the general oversight of the college (Gmelch, Wolverton, Wolverton, and Sarros, 1999). Finally, recruiting, hiring, and developing the best faculty and chairs affect the academic environment and advance the college's reputation (W. E. Gardner, 1992). In short, the living legacy of a dean resides in the faculty hired under his/her tenure.

In addition, deans take on the decidedly business-oriented functions of seeking new student markets, finding opportunities to combine academic interests with business or industrial interests, monitoring external grant opportunities, searching for developments outside their units, and representing their units to off-campus agencies and alumni. In essence, they market their colleges (Creswell and England, 1994; M. R. Hall, 1993). Such a comprehensive list of role requirements does indeed suggest a transition in the deanship from chief academic officer to chief executive officer (Creswell and England, 1994; Tucker and Bryan, 1988).

This expansion of a dean's fiscal and managerial roles has not diminished the expectation that he/she keep current in his/her academic discipline. Upper-level administrators want deans to become scholar-leaders who model the behaviors most desired among faculty. Similarly, faculty expect deans to retain their credibility as former faculty members, which for the most part happens when deans conduct research and publish. An interesting disjuncture occurs for some deans who continue to engage in research. To gain the stature generally associated with advanced faculty rank, they conducted discipline-specific studies and experiments. To retain a research agenda after taking the deanship, many reorient their research projects to focus on organizational concerns they face as deans (Grace, 1982). Although deans continue to do research, faculty sometimes deem these new endeavors to be substandard to past efforts.

The Reality of Today's Deanship
Because the academic deanship was not a preconceived notion but a response to growing pressures on college and university presidents, it evolved rather

haphazardly, "largely without focus or direction" (Tucker and Bryan, 1988, p. 3). The result today, especially in large universities with large colleges, is an ill-defined midmanagerial position (Gould, 1964; Stein and Trachtenberg, 1993). Stripped of some of their original aura of power (with the inception of the provost) but delegated more responsibility, deans now seem to elicit criticism as "consequential but frequently ineffective" (Coladarci, 1980; Fagin, 1997; Morsink, 1987).

In 1993, Martin conducted case studies of deans from varying disciplines in an attempt to profile an "effective academic dean." The responses given by these deans attest to the expanded role of the dean. Martin's deans had the ability to convey ideas and information to and from the college and community. They also described themselves as "managers," "planner/analysts," and "advocates," all of which define expertise in areas that involve interacting with people inside and outside the university. As administrative experts, these deans perceived themselves as visible and participative, and working toward a collective vision.

A further descriptor, "cultural representative," suggests that deans personify the culture of colleges and universities. As the primary conveyors of society's overall culture, colleges and universities must ensure that the cultural properties of their institutions are clearly understood by not only their students but also their faculty, administration, and the society, which ultimately reaps its benefits (Bergquist, 1992, citing Parsons and Platt). As the university's agent, the dean is charged with representing its cultural base.

In attempting to meet this expectation, deans run up against an inherent conflict in the system. On the one hand, professors form a community of self-regulated scholars. On the other, presidents seek to exert institutional control directed at social change. Deans become mediators in this conflict with no clear guidelines to govern their conduct (Mayhew, 1957). In essence, as the external duties of presidents expanded, the task of reconciling faculty autonomy with the broader charge for social change passed from presidents to deans (Gould, 1964). Held accountable, at least in part, for realizing the university's societal role, deans experienced pressures to prove, by the numbers, that their colleges were indeed contributing to the greater good. This expectation continues today. The rub comes in the difficulty experienced in trying to quantify faculty contributions to universities, which tend to be qualitative in nature (Ginzberg, 1959).

In today's academy, "culture" carries multiple meanings. The inner workings of universities consist of multiple subcultures—collegial, managerial, political, bureaucratic, and organizational anarchy, to name a few—that coalesce, conflict, and coexist with each (Bensimon, Neumann, and Birnbaum, 1989; Bergquist, 1992; Morgan, 1980). Two systemic phenomena weave these cultures together. The first relates to the use of power and authority, the second to a dual-ranking feature, which governs the source of power. In the former instance, deans work within the rules and regulations of university bureaucracies to carry out their routine administrative tasks. When it comes to meeting more general societal goals, however, they lack the control over faculty that is normally associated with the employer/employee relationship characteristic of most bureaucracies. This situation occurs primarily because of the autonomy that faculty assert in the pursuit of academic freedom. Instead, deans must negotiate with and build consensus among professionals who need little supervision but require support, protection, and sometimes direction, especially as it pertains to melding the pursuits of academic freedom with overarching societal goals (Merz, 1999; Mintzberg, 1998). In the end, faculty cannot be supervised, administered, or directed but must be coordinated and led (Euwema, 1961).

The latter cultural mechanism, dual rankings, derives from a systemic peculiarity. Universities dictate deans' hierarchical positions and rank, as they do for other faculty, but credibility within one's discipline comes from outside the local university and is based on research and publication records. And herein lies the bind. Effective administration and scholarship both take time, personal and professional commitment, and dedication; any effort to engage in one often comes at the expense of the other (Creswell and England, 1994). With respect to dealing with faculty, much of a dean's power is tied to his/her academic status rather than his/her assigned hierarchical position. Deans in most cases simply cannot exercise authority over faculty through edict. They in effect hold no direct recourse over tenured faculty who choose to follow their own personal directives instead of those generated by the university. Historically, the resolution of this matter has manifested itself in a system of vague and incomplete rules and unwritten procedures, which vary across discipline, time, and institution (Caplow and McGee, 1958). Tenure, promotion, and contract termination are good examples of this phenomenon.

To complicate matters further, a college's disparate cultures, even when goals are agreed upon in general, often engage in antagonistic relationships within the context of the university. For example, an externally generated goal that is promoted by central administration may require that colleges improve educational quality as measured by increases in student retention and graduation rates. Faculty, however, may decide that the way to achieve this goal is by increasing course rigor, which very likely could result in higher attrition and lower graduation rates. Indeed, when a university lacks agreement among its cultures—a collective "glue," so to speak (Bergquist, 1992)—its deans may find themselves mired in bureaucratic stalemates among warring factions. It is no wonder, then, that the position suffers a high turnover rate (Twombly, 1992).

As administrators, deans must function in an environment that is subsumed within the greater university environment.

Role Conflict and Ambiguity

Such dichotomous situations can lead to misunderstandings, misplaced priorities, and misalignment between deans and their colleges. As administrators, deans must function in an environment that is subsumed within the greater university environment. Ryan (1980) refers to this phenomenon as operating a professional bureaucracy (the college) within a professional bureaucracy (the university). As a consequence, deans hold legitimate authority granted by the university but are sometimes unable to assert it within the context of the college. Thus, as a university's demands increase, deans are compelled to maintain credibility in the eyes of faculty who deny any assertion of that authority (M. Wolverton, Wolverton, and Gmelch, 1999). When they are able to effectively maintain this balance, deans are considered to be in control. When they are not, they experience disequilibrium (A. E. Austin, 1984; Drennan, 1983).

The dean's dilemma is a very real one. "[He/she] is usually the one expected to lead the college to bigger and better things—few deans are hired with the mandate to maintain the status quo. [Such a] dilemma presents a ready-made tension between the dean and the faculty" (Yarger, 1998, p. 141). A dean's use of time exacerbates this tension. As researchers, deans have years of practice at reserving judgment, of taking time to make decisions. As deans, they must now ration time by prioritizing and delegating. If deans are unable to do so, they become bogged down in busywork, which on the one hand releases them from the necessity of thinking (Gould, 1964) but on the other results in role conflict and role ambiguity (M. C. Cohen and March, 1974; March, 1988; March and Olsen, 1979).

Role conflicts arise when deans must engage in situations that conflict with their value systems or are in conflict with each other (Rizzo, House, and Lirtzman, 1970; M. Wolverton, Wolverton, and Gmelch, 1999). As demands and expectations are increasingly heaped upon deans, there is dissonance between the intent or desired outcomes of the various factions who promulgate them (Bowker, 1982a). For example, a directive to cut departmental costs may be countermanded by a faculty demand to increase such costs. Each player has its own justification for such demands, and thus the task of trying to satisfy both constituencies becomes difficult (M. Wolverton, Wolverton, and Gmelch, 1999). The closer deans identify with faculty and think of themselves as faculty members who happen to be carrying out administrative duties, the greater the role conflict experienced (Bowker, 1982a; Kapel and Dejnozka, 1979; M. Wolverton, Wolverton, and Gmelch, 1999).

When information that is necessary to an organization's effectiveness is withheld or not available, role ambiguity results. Thus, if deans receive no clear guidelines about budget priorities, decisions made at the college level may seem capricious and indefensible. Such ambiguity results in dissatisfaction, anxiety over the role, and ineffectual performance (Rizzo, House, and Lirtzman, 1970). Indeed, research has borne out that low job satisfaction and commitment to the organization and a high level of job stress result from excessive role conflict and role ambiguity (Kahn, Wolfe, Quinn, and Snoek, 1964; R. A. Scott, 1979).

Dean Stress

In work environments, desirable stress levels promote greater work effort and enhance performance. Perceived success, rising to a challenge, taking advantage of an opportunity, and improving oneself are all reactions to positive stressors (Brewer, 1995; Gmelch and Chan, 1994; Ivancevich and Matteson, 1987; Lewis, Garcia, and Jobs, 1990). Debilitating stress leads to excessive physical and mental strain, impaired job performance, and dissatisfaction (Caplan, 1983; Caplan and others, 1980; Dawis, 1994; Dawis, England, and Lofquist, 1964; Dawis and Lofquist, 1984; Day and Bedeian, 1995; Holland, 1966; R. L. Kahn, 1981; R. Kahn and Byosiere, 1992; Kulik, Oldham, and Hackman, 1987; Robbins, Schmitt, Ehinger, and Welliver, 1994).

A recent study found that seven stress dimensions capture much of the stress deans experience on the job (Gmelch, Wolverton, Wolverton, and Sarros, 1999). Administrative Task Stress, which appears to account for most of the deans' work-related stress, arises from pressures that surround daily operations. Especially troublesome aspects of the job include meeting deadlines, attending meetings, keeping up with paperwork, preparing budgets, and dealing with interruptions. These stressors are longstanding. Forty years ago, deans bemoaned the heavy toll of such "housekeeping" chores, such as report writing (Gmelch, Wolverton, Wolverton, and Sarros, 1999; Gould, 1964).

Tensions between deans and upper management manifest themselves in Provost-Related Stress. Deans express frustration over trying to resolve differences with their provosts, having insufficient authority to perform their responsibilities, and not knowing how they are evaluated. This type of stress also seems to be consistent over time. In studies conducted during the past twenty years, researchers have found incompatibility with superiors to be one of the major causes for deans' leaving their positions (Gmelch, Wolverton, Wolverton, and Sarros, 1999; Otis and Caragonne, 1979; Robbins, Schmitt, Ehinger, and Welliver, 1994).

Faculty/Chair-Related Stress reveals the conflict-ridden nature of academic administrator positions. This stress emanates partially from having to evaluate staff and make promotion and tenure decisions. Time/Personal Stress stems from after-hour activities, such as work-related social obligations, travel, and the competition for time between the dean's personal and professional lives. For decades, deans have complained about the encroachment of work on their personal time. One-third of the deans in Gould's study said they had too little time to take even a one-week vacation. And, to a certain extent, strife between faculty and deans and time issues contributed to the exodus of social work deans in the 1970s (Gmelch, Wolverton, Wolverton, and Sarros, 1999; Gould, 1964; P. M. Miller, 1989; Otis and Caragonne, 1979).

Scholarship Stress occurs because deans have insufficient time to stay current in their academic field or make progress in their academic careers and find it difficult to balance their leadership and scholarship responsibilities. One dean in Gould's study went so far as to suggest that the academic deanship is "a distinct career and a person taking this position should pretty much say farewell to scholarship. He can do little teaching [or research] and even this is done on the run" (Gould, 1964, p. 43; Koch, 1968). In the overall scheme, deans have little time to engage in the kind of research that commands disciplinary respect. In the past, they continued research endeavors to avoid the disdain faculty reserved for administrators. Today, deans feel compelled to set an example by keeping their research interests alive (Gmelch, Wolverton, Wolverton, and Sarros, 1999; Gould, 1964).

Deans who believe that they receive insufficient compensation and recognition for their administrative and scholarly performance experience Salary/Recognition Stress (Gmelch, Wolverton, Wolverton, and Sarros, 1999). This stressor has existed for some time. Both Gould (1964) and Bowker's deans (1982a) alluded to some dissatisfaction with salaries, and others claim that financial remuneration is a primary motivator for considering the position in the first place (Lamborn, 1991). Finally, Fundraising Stress points to current pressures on deans to engage in fundraising and financial support activities (Gmelch, Wolverton, Wolverton, and Sarros, 1999). Again, these stressors are not new. Such fiscal responsibilities, along with budgeting, were primary reasons that deans of schools of social work resigned in the 1970s (Otis and Caragonne, 1979).

Each of these types of dean stress can be influenced in some way by numerous personal or work-related variables. For example, older deans experience higher levels of administrative task, provost-related, and fundraising stress but lower levels of faculty-related, time/personal, and scholarship stress. Experience also seems to impact stress. The longer deans have been in their positions, the lower their levels of administrative task and fundraising stress. They do, however, exhibit higher levels of salary/recognition stress. Both women and deans of color tend toward lower levels of faculty-related stress. Women, however, experience higher levels of administrative task stress and deans of color higher provost-related stress. And if deans hold high self-expectations, they increase their administrative task, faculty-related, and time/personal stress levels. Work-related variables that seem to add to most stress categories include role conflict, role ambiguity, dealing with new technology, handling student conflicts, and promoting diversity (M. Wolverton, Gmelch, and Wolverton, 2000).

A Final Reality: A Lack of Preparation for Deans

Over time, "the idea that individuals can be deliberately prepared for administration at the college level [has been] relatively . . . controversial" (Bauer, 1955, p. 5). Less than one-third of Gould's liberal arts deans believed that formal administrative training was desirable. Most asserted that an essential part of their administrative preparation came from being faculty members. About 70 percent imagined that experience as a chair might help. Others added that committee work provided an arena for learning about administration. One-half of them suggested that an apprenticeship to a dean would be desirable. Most thought that deans could prepare themselves by reading about higher education administration (Gould, 1964). In contrast, deans of nursing called for formal preparation of deans (George and Deets, 1983; B. A. Hall, de Tornyay, and Mitsunaga, 1983; Kibrick, 1980).

During the past twenty-five years, a fair number of education and law deans had some previous management or professional experience outside the academy. Law deans, for instance, had worked as lawyers (82 percent), for the government (52.4 percent), or in business (34 percent) (Abramson and Moss, 1977). Education deans with prior experience had been school principals or superintendents or college department chairs. All had been faculty members. This administrative and professional experience did not seem to provide adequate preparation and training for the job, however. Most deans studied have at one time or another commented that they had been insufficiently prepared for the deanship (Abramson and Moss, 1977; Gould, 1964; Griffiths and McCarty, 1980; Thiessen and Howey, 1998). Even so, deans often failed to engage in any type of self-development exercises in the year previous to the study, whether academically oriented or related to tasks they encountered as deans. For instance, a large portion of education deans studied in 1980 believed that more training in areas such as group facilitation, decision making, and budgeting would have been useful, but only one-third had sought any help. Women in general reported needing assistance in leadership development. Deans at research universities felt particularly ill-prepared to deal with the power relations that permeated their institutions (Griffiths and McCarty, 1980).

Today, the issue still seems very much alive and well. Townsend and Bassoppo-Moyo (1996) found that even though deans could compile long lists of requisite skills and traits, few had formal, specialized training for the position. In their 1996 study of 210 academic deans, they identified five competencies—technical, contextual, interpersonal, communicative, and conceptual—in which deans desired but frequently lacked skills and knowledge. Technical competency refers specifically to administrative tasks, such as budgeting and finance. Deans who possess contextual competency understand the higher education administration environment. Interpersonal competence involves maintenance of relationships with and among people through such activities as team building and conflict resolution. Communication includes effective use of both traditional and technological modes. Finally, deans who are competent conceptually have a grasp of the theoretical underpinnings of higher education (Townsend and Bassoppo-Moyo, 1996).

Study findings clearly indicated a specific need for better preparation in fiscal management, law, and use of computers. In general, it appears that a growing number of people who fill the position do not possess the skills and background knowledge necessary for effective performance. At a minimum, universities find that they must train ineffective deans on the job. In reality, such situations may cause universities to suffer the consequences of having selected the wrong person (Townsend and Bassoppo-Moyo, 1996).

What Challenges Do Deans Face?

WE NOW HAVE A SOMEWHAT clearer picture of most academic deans. Most deans are white, middle-aged males, with the notable exception of nursing deans. We sense that increasingly deans face challenges that lie outside their spheres of experience, a situation with a long history. Scholar-deans of the 1960s were charged with raising the level of education quality by challenging their more able students while at the same time expanding access to large numbers of students who were academically unprepared for college. They faced accusations of curricular irrelevancy and mandates to study, revise, and weed out weak programs and to initiate new honors and interdisciplinary ones. Low salaries and unfavorable working conditions spurred faculty unrest. And a new era of standards-based accreditation posed the necessity for expensive, time-consuming self-studies (Gould, 1964). Law deans a decade later fought against insufficient funding and complained about inadequate classroom facilities, faculty competence, and student morale (Abramson and Moss, 1977). In the 1980s, nursing deans saw budgeting and funding, external demands, planning, college structure and administration, faculty needs, recruitment and retention of minority students, and the use of technology as major issues (Prock, 1981, 1983; Spero, 1983).

Today, we believe that, although all deans face discipline-specific challenges, some issues remain systemic and common ground exists across their experiences. Further, the challenges delineated by deans in the NSAD study for the most part are non-discipline-specific issues, which all deans face. When these deans were asked to comment on the three greatest challenges they faced in the next three to five years, seven categories of anticipated challenges emerged. Prominent among them were strained fiscal resources, externally imposed accountability pressures, demands for relevant curricula and programs, technology advancement and educational delivery, faculty ill equipped to meet student and system demands, diversity, and professional and personal imbalance (Wolverton, Montez, and Gmelch, 2000). Interestingly, deans did not note many of the traditionally recognized responsibilities of the position such as hiring, tenure, and promotion unless they impacted a college's ability to respond to students' and society's needs.[4]

More than 75 percent of the deans agreed that the fiscal, accountability (among other administrative concerns), and curriculum and program development challenges were the three most important. Almost 30 percent of all respondents to this question rated fiscal challenges number one. About 14 percent suggested faculty issues as paramount; fewer mentioned technology (5 percent), personal balance (3 percent), or diversity (2 percent) as top choices. As a group, these challenges emanate from a rapidly evolving higher education landscape. In each arena, the juxtaposition of the traditional models of the deanship, expectations of the faculty, and the realities of the role marks the critical challenges of today's dean.

Fiscal Constraints and Demands for Accountability

Skepticism as to its societal value and a general sense of distrust about spending practices and educational outcomes have affected the availability of resources to expand programs demanded by the increasingly diverse populations served. From a governmental perspective, shifts in funding for higher education are not being viewed as leading to inadequate resources but as changes in priorities (Frances, Pumerantz, and Caplan, 1999; Zemsky and Wagner, 1997). Competing social problems, such as crime, racial inequality, and health and welfare, make it difficult for institutions of higher education to secure a significant portion of available public funds (California Higher Education Policy Center, 1994; Marcus, 1997; Mortenson, 1994c; Stanton, 1990).

In demonstrating a reluctance to tax themselves at high enough levels to adequately support higher education, citizens have signaled a change in belief. Higher education is increasingly viewed as a private good that should be paid for by those individuals who directly benefit from it ("A Little Learning," 1997). Proponents of this new understanding of higher education suggest that any public good derived from higher education will survive because of the actions of individuals (E. Cohen and Geske, 1990; Mortenson, 1994a). The resulting decrease in funding experienced by many universities makes infrastructure and capital upkeep fiscally debilitating (Association of Governing Boards of Universities and Colleges, 1996).

Calls for educational and fiscal accountability, another consequence of the shifting political climate, often exist side by side with reductions in or reallocations of resources. Such externally imposed constraints force universities to cut costs at every turn while at the same time expecting colleges to initiate new programs that will provide accountability measures and nullify public skepticism (Marcus, 1997). Deans, who are in the role of budgeter and financier, end up in the middle of funding struggles. Fundraising and FTE generation, swathed in the language of cost efficiency, push deans into the realm of management and drive a wedge between them and faculty whose perceptions of what constitutes a university education (and research) remain at odds with monetary and competitive mandates.

These business-initiated directives for reform coupled with directives from taxpayers to raise the quality of education require resources, some of which do not exist. The most common solution, soliciting corporate gifts and other forms of external funding, requires that deans actively participate in a vicious cycle of first seeking money, the procurement of which depends directly on prescribed curricular reform. They then must convince faculty to engage in such reforms with the hope of being able to attract more money, which as often as not is tied to more prescriptive reforms. Faculty draw lines between what is skill-based training and what is theory-based education (Jacobson, 1994). They fear that universities in the quest for financial support may evolve into overgrown technical schools (R. M. Davis, 1985). Deans, playing the dual role of fundraiser and faculty advocate, must strike a balance between corporate expectations for the development of skills and faculty beliefs that education embraces more than skills.

On perhaps a more ominous note, corporate demands increasingly creep into, and potentially taint, the very essence of the university—basic research. Indeed, "commercially sponsored research," Press and Washburn (2000, p. 39) assert, "is putting at risk the paramount value of higher education—disinterested inquiry. . . . [Alarmingly], universities are behaving more and more like for-profit companies." Universities counter by arguing that increasing the number of patents registered 20 years ago from 250 to almost 5,000 in today's market has led to the production of important new products for consumers.

But consider the following reality: In 1998, the Department of Plant and Microbial Biology at Berkeley entered into an agreement with a Swiss pharmaceutical company. In exchange for $25 million, the firm received first right to licensure on nearly one-third of the department's discoveries, including the results of research funded by state and federal sources. The company also now holds two of five seats on the department's research committee, which determines how the money is spent and when research findings are released. Berkeley justifies such moves by pointing to decreases from 50 percent to 34 percent of its overall budget in public funding over the last decade. It claims that without the laboratory facilities and access to commercially developed proprietary databases, which accompany private funding, Berkeley could neither provide first-rate graduate education nor perform the fundamental research that is part of its mission (Press and Washburn, 2000).

This view has become more and more the norm, as universities across the country turn to private sector businesses for larger portions of their research dollars. The question becomes whether the Berkeleys of the world are sacrificing research for the public good (a hallmark of the academy) for private profit (Press and Washburn, 2000). The controversy is ripe, and the debate about private good versus public good will loom large for many deans. How we view higher education in this country in the future may well depend on how current deans rise to the occasion. Will higher education be seen as a means to an end or as an end in and of itself?

Demands for Curricular Relevance

The Hudson Institute estimates that 52 percent of new entrants into the labor force will require one or more years of college education (Kerr, 1994), but the business sector has become increasingly dissatisfied with the skills and abilities possessed by college graduates. Businesses invest more than $60 billion annually in education and training in the workplace (Eurich, 1990). Convinced that they are spending money to provide training they assumed already existed—namely, a college education—America's disillusioned corporations have begun to develop in-house mini-universities (Thompson, 2000). This new breed of further education competes with current business administration programs offered at colleges and universities (Allen, 1996). As a consequence, efforts to regain corporate support and student enrollment drive curriculum reform at many universities today (Cantor, 2000).

Changes in higher education reflect a need to accommodate a changing student populace, respond to competition among educational providers, and deal with issues of access (Kaplan, 2000; A. E. Levine, 2000; S. C. Smith and Piele, 1997). Moreover, multiple facets of today's work world demand that stronger ties be established between the educational and practice systems (Curry and Wergin, 1993). For example, corporate America wants people who can work in teams, professions such as engineering and computer science want workers with up-to-date skills and knowledge, and the general public cries out for better teacher and administrative preparation for K–12 schools. Carried to the extreme, such changes could alter the meaning of the college degree to the point where students emerge from colleges with competency transcripts outlining their information knowledge and acquired skills. As trends move toward standardization of educational achievement, deans face the unenviable task of trying to define and offer curricula that bridge old traditions and new expectations (A. E. Levine, 2000).

Technical Advancements and Educational Delivery Systems

Conservatively, advancements in technology double every two years. This change, coupled with changes in student populations, competition between institutions, and state mandates, creates a constant need for higher education to keep current (D. I. Barker, 1994; Batson and Bass, 1996; Frances, Pumerantz, and Caplan, 1999; K. C. Green, 1996; Privateer, 1999; Van Dusen, 1997). At one end of the spectrum, information technology has "emerged as a permanent, respected, and increasingly essential component of the college experience" (K. C. Green, 1996, p. 24). Evidence of technology encroachment in the academy is clear. A recent study about course delivery found that more than one-half of current college courses use e-mail as a form of regular class correspondence—a 20 percent increase over the past five years. Additionally, 40 percent of these courses use Web-based resources, and more than 25 percent employ Web page technology (Murray, 2000).

At the other end of the spectrum, public officials, enamored with information technology, have declared that "the last campus college has been built" (Merisotis and Phipps, 1999, p.13; Noam, 1995; Perelman, 1993) and that university teaching will be replaced by "knowledge industries, which can deliver needed, just-in-time knowledge to workers [with] no [need for] formal university training" (Eamon, 1999, p. 200). Deans recognize the dilemma they face. Once concerned primarily with professional identity, continued learning, and career advancement (Stark, Lowther, and Hagerty, 1986), they now rank dealing with technology use in their colleges among their top challenges (Wolverton, Montez, and Gmelch, 2000; Townsend and Bassoppo-Moyo, 1996; Van Dusen, 1997).

To be sure, technical advancements help drive curricular reform, in terms of both content and delivery. In fact, computer industry commercials and magazine advertisements bombard the public with images of technology and learning coexisting in the educational process. The result is a belief that education via technology is easy, broadly accessible, expedient, and accommodating and that it opens "new dimensions" to learning (Baker and Gloster, 1994; Barnard, 1997). As a consequence, the public wants high quality, low costs, and convenience (A. W. Astin, 1993; Carnegie Foundation, 1990; Committee C, 1996; Van Dusen, 2000).

In response to these expectations, proprietary institutions such as the University of Phoenix and Athena University compete with traditional colleges and universities for students on the basis of course relevance and delivery convenience (Cantor, 2000; Van Dusen, 2000; Welsh, 2000). The University of Phoenix, an accredited institution that offers baccalaureate, master's, and doctoral degrees, targets working professionals with work-specific curricula delivered in the evenings and on weekends (University of Phoenix, 1999). Athena

University, a university offering on-line courses only, boasts a liberal arts, interdisciplinary curriculum that emphasizes the "development of critical thinking skills" and the "free exchange of ideas in a nonphysical setting" (Athena University, 1999).

Similarly, some traditional universities have developed extensive telecommunication networks specifically designed to serve constituents in outlying areas. Administrative commitments to maintain competitiveness in light of current technological trends and to provide wider access to educational opportunities have fostered initiatives to develop on-line courses and distance learning programs. For instance, the governors of eleven western states have endorsed the development of a public, virtual university to serve their region (Johnstone and Krauth, 1996). More recently, Universitas 21, a network of eighteen prominent universities in ten countries, revealed a proposal to deliver new curricula, courseware, and delivery platforms for technology-based education (Maslen, 2000).

Rapid growth of these programs and universities has raised concerns among faculty about program quality and educational value. In fact, some research shows students' performance in technology-based classrooms does not differ from that of students who attend face-to-face lectures (Russell, 1998; Wang and Newlin, 2000). Other studies, however, suggest that the cognitive impact of technology on learning varies across student groups (Flowers, Pascarella, and Pierson, 2000; Wolfe, 2001). In the end, we must ask whether an at-a-distance or virtual education experience is at least equivalent to that found at traditional colleges and universities (Eamon, 1999; Management Practice Institute, 1997; Sperling and Tucker, 1997).

As institutions explore their role in this emerging paradigm, deans juggle institutional technology plans with faculty concerns about whether "virtual" components reflect progressive education or no education at all. Indeed, faculty believe that the Athena universities of the world try to sell something that cannot exist outside a physical learning environment (Johnstone and Krauth, 1996). At New York University, for instance, faculty, carrying signs that read "televisions don't teach, people do" and "clone sheep, not Internet courses," picketed against perceived pressures to develop on-line courses (Eamon, 1999).

LIBRARY
COLBY-SAWYER COLLEGE
NEW LONDON, NH 03257

These faculty believe and engage in time-honored educational traditions and means of instruction that seem in conflict with the cognitive potentials of current information technologies that allow for compressed time lines, weekend sessions, and delivery via teleconferencing (Latta, 1996; Privateer, 1999). The problem for deans lies not so much in the existence of these pressures themselves but in the rapidity with which technologies change and the resistance with which some faculty greet this change.

The Diversity of Shifting Demographics

Currently, an estimated 50 percent of the U.S. population attends college at some point in their lives (Kerr, 1994). If present enrollment trends continue, projections suggest that in ten years 60 percent of the 18- to 21-year-old cohort will engage in some form of postsecondary education. In fact, this population is predicted to increase by nearly 1 million over the next five years (Frances, Pumerantz, and Caplan, 1999). While record numbers of traditionally aged people (18 to 24 years of age) will attend college, increasing numbers of older community members are joining the college ranks as well (Frances, Pumerantz, and Caplan, 1999; Sperling and Tucker, 1997; Taylor and Massy, 1996). Many enroll part time, work, and have families with children living at home. By 1995, more than one-quarter of all college students worked full time, more than one-half worked at least part time, almost one-half were older than 25 years of age, and 43 percent attended part time. By 1998, fewer than 20 percent of enrollees fit the traditional collegiate archetype (18 to 22 years old, attending full time, living on campus) (A. Levine and Cureton, 1998). And enrollment projections for older adults in the 35- to 64-year-old age groups suggest substantial increases in the near future (Frances, Pumerantz, and Caplan, 1999).

Each of these subpopulations—traditional and older students—is also changing, with more racial and ethnic minorities and women matriculating into undergraduate and graduate degree programs (Aguirre, 2000). Currently, students from historically underrepresented populations attend colleges and universities at a much higher rate than at any other time in the history of U.S. education (Kerr, 1994; A. Levine and Cureton, 1998; Murdock and Hoque,

1999). In fact, more than one-half of today's students are women (A. Levine and Cureton, 1998). Similarly, during the last decade, increases in the enrollment of Hispanic and Asians made up for decreases in the enrollment numbers of white 18- to 24-year-olds and a slight decline in African Americans. Current state initiatives and lawsuits that question the necessity of affirmative action raise concerns that over the next few years there will be a "crowding out of minority youth by growing white youth enrollments, potentially rolling back decades of progress [made] toward broadening educational opportunities" (Frances, Pumerantz, and Caplan, 1999, p. 28).

Faculty-Student-System Incongruence

Shifting demographics, market demands, and technical advances work together against deans and create mismatches in priorities, capabilities, and capacity. In the first case, younger students, well versed in computer-based delivery systems, expect faculty to engage them in learning activities via e-mail, news groups, bulletin boards, listservs, and chat rooms. They enjoy participating in a shared on-line environment (Brown and Duguid, 1996; Eamon, 1999). They experiment, participate in social learning, and multiprocess, reading, listening to music, using the computer simultaneously. Many have relatively short attentions spans (Brown, 2000). For this cohort raised on immediacy and MTV, classes in which instructors engage students in active learning are avoided, poorly evaluated, and openly challenged by students (Latta, 1996).

Older adults return to college or start advanced degree programs to change careers or secure advancements in their current line of work (Kerr, 1994; Mortenson, 1994b). These mature students expect a closer relationship between what they learn in the classroom and its applicability to their job or career (D. K. Scott and Awbrey, 1993).

In addition, minority student populations expect to have mentors in the faculty and administration who look like them and will be committed to supporting their educational efforts. If universities are to respond to their expectations, it will have an impact on general faculty and administrative hiring practices and doctoral program admissions policies (Burgos-Sasscer, 1990). Additionally, this population of students is generating grassroots curricular reform, which advocates the integration of American diversity courses into university program-of-study requirements (Kerr, 1994). The goal of these students is to move ethnic study programs from marginalized positions as add-ons in established departments to stand alone departments and majors (A. Levine and Cureton, 1998). Such reforms require that colleges allocate money to expand their programs and seek faculty qualified to teach the courses. Inevitably, changing faculty demographics and restructuring curricula also place cultural demands on colleges, which ultimately fall squarely on the shoulders of deans.

Institutional efforts to retain nontraditional student populations have generated conversations about the expectations of faculty. The debate centers on faculty accessibility to students versus faculty commitments to personal scholarship and research. Studies show that faculty have a significant influence on students' satisfaction and subsequently on student retention (A. W. Astin, 1993). The reward structure for faculty, however, emphasizes research and scholarly work that often prevents them from establishing meaningful connections with students outside the classroom. "As a consequence, faculty, particularly junior faculty, spend little time with undergraduate students and in university service" (Kuh and Whitt, 1988, p. 16).

This situation again places deans directly in the middle between faculty who are reluctant to cut into precious research and writing time and students who readily voice their dissatisfaction to central administration. In essence, deans must mediate between a faculty governance system for tenure that reinforces research and scholarship, upper administration's expectations and concerns about student retention, and students' desires for more faculty interaction and broader minority representation (A. W. Astin, 1993; Kuh and Whitt, 1988). Each priority places demands on limited resources. Deans must make sense of these vying interests with little direction or clear institutional positions.

A more sensitive, student-related issue revolves around the environment itself and points to further mismatches in the system. At universities across the country, campus climates are politically correct but not necessarily conducive to learning for minority groups. Student groups polarize along racial and ethnic lines and do not socialize with each other. Civility has declined, classroom disruptions are up almost 50 percent, and faculty complaints about classroom situations are on the rise. Sexual harassment has also increased. In this type of environment, many students, regardless of race or gender, feel uncomfortable raising controversial topics and expressing unpopular views. Instead, faculty and students increasingly disengage, coming to campus only for classes. In effect, deans face the challenge of translating what some see as idle rhetoric into hospitable campus environments (A. Levine and Cureton, 1998; Stage and Manning, 1992).

Market forces complicate matters further. Expectations of the labor market have shifted enrollments heavily to professional schools and away from colleges of humanities and social sciences. Any university attempting to meet corporate demands encourages a redistribution of faculty to professional programs, fueling internal tensions between traditional liberal arts and market-driven, business-oriented disciplines. The capabilities of existing faculty often lie, however, in disciplines that simply do not spark demand. Deans in such situations vie for resources to maintain existing programs and to create new ones at one and the same time.

Finally, the students that colleges hope to attract are technologically sophisticated (Batson and Bass, 1996; K. C. Green, 1997). They expect on-line libraries, video production facilities, virtual classrooms complete with teleconferencing equipment and multimedia capacities, high-speed data networks, and high-quality, interactive Web sites comparable to those they experience through cable and satellite programs or by surfing the Web (Van Dusen, 1997). Acclimated to the technology and savvy in its use they may be, but serving up cut-and-pasted information in a glitzy Power Point presentation cannot camouflage a lack of demonstrated understanding or ability to synthesize material. In the end, we might ask whether these students are truly sophisticated thinkers who will be able to successfully navigate the perils of the real work world (Tell, 2000).

As this drama unfolds, deans find themselves straddling a gap. On the one hand, central administration expects technology to be incorporated into instructional pedagogies and used to broaden the access to their institutions. On the other, the institutional capacity simply does not exist. As a result, deans increasingly must search for the financial wherewithal to provide a technical infrastructure (hardware, software, technical assistance, and training) that becomes outdated in months, not years.

Faculty define their instructional mission in terms of what students know. Today's students define it in terms of how they experience learning and whether what they learn ultimately aids them in finding a job (K. C. Green, 1999). If current faculty cannot meet industry needs, deans with limited vacant or new faculty lines may find their colleges at a disadvantage when it comes to fulfilling students' expectations (Kerr, 1994). Realizing a happy medium between knowledge for knowledge's sake and learning work-related skills requires that deans find the time for faculty to retool, provide them with the resources to do so, and convince them that such shifts are in everybody's best interest (Brown, 2000).

Issues of Balance

Three issues of balance—personal/professional, scholarship/leadership, and long term/short term—seem to dominate the lives of deans. Achieving balance means making choices and enjoying those choices. One of the significant stressors in the work lives of deans revolves around trying to strike a balance between their professional and personal lives (Friedman, Christensen, and DeGroot, 1998; Gmelch, Wolverton, and Wolverton, 1999; Gmelch, Wolverton, Wolverton, and Sarros, 1999). The administrative arm of the academy functions under expectations biased by an unwritten code. Simply put, career advancement often goes to those who put in long hours at work and allocate additional time to university and college social activities. Being seen becomes the ultimate criterion for ascension in the ranks. This infringement on deans' privacy is a high stressor in their lives (M. Wolverton, Gmelch, and Wolverton, 2000). Stressed out deans typically work their personal lives right out of existence. Even on vacation, they have to be busy to feel okay, checking in with the office, working on reports that can wait or be written by someone else. Deans with career aspirations want to be seen as driving forces. Taken to the extreme, deans sacrifice personal intuition, judgment, and integrity to political dexterity. Time spent relaxing or just plain having fun is time ill spent in the eyes of guilt-ridden deans.

In their everyday work lives, deans also face a philosophical dilemma that demands that they place relative values on their roles as scholars and their responsibilities as leaders. Universities often hire deans for their scholarly endeavors and research reputations. In fact, Cronin and Crawford (1999) suggest that deans must be well read and published in their area of expertise to be taken seriously by faculty. The message sent reflects an expectation of continued scholarly work. But the arena into which deans are thrust does not support the realization of such expectations. Deans rapidly move from a professional life built on long periods of contemplation and writing to calendars filled with fifteen-minute time slots and days crammed with meeting upon meeting, week after week. In reality, they become casualties of someone else's agenda (Sarros and Gmelch, 1996).

Conventional wisdom suggests that people change their behavior to match their beliefs. So if deans believe that their continued involvement in scholarly activities is important, they will make time for it. In reality, people adjust their belief systems to match current behaviors. They rationalize. Deans tell themselves, "Daily administrative tasks must be done, and I'm the one who has to do them." Guilt becomes a common bedfellow of scholar-deans. Although they have reprioritized their roles, weighing in in favor of administrative responsibilities, they have not done away with the stress associated with research activities. These deans seek to mitigate a tension between remaining true to their scholarship and properly performing as administrators (Grace, 1982; Mintzberg, 1998). Their highest priorities as faculty members become their least important tasks as deans, precisely because they are time-consuming, long-term efforts (Gmelch and Chan, 1994; M. Wolverton, Gmelch, and Wolverton, 2000).

A third issue of balance, realizing long-term agendas while engaging in short-term tasks, revolves around how deans conduct college business. Daily to-dos of running a college, such as keeping records, filing reports, and dealing

Deans rapidly move from a professional life built on long periods of contemplation and writing to calendars filled with fifteen-minute time slots and days crammed with meeting upon meeting, week after week.

with personnel squabbles, wage war against "what we're all about." Deans are constantly held to standards of compliance and conformity but receive signals that encourage raising the research productivity of college faculty, increasing the quality of programs, and diversifying the faculty, students, and staff, all of which require a degree of creativity and innovation. The deadlines associated with operational tasks often project a sense of urgency, which compounds the problem further. Such artificial urgency eats away precious time that could be devoted to more important tasks. For instance, reports with filing deadlines, which ultimately form one layer of a pile on someone's desk in central administration, create a sense of urgency that may not exist. Technical conveniences, such as voice and e-mail, can seduce deans into the same subjective line of reasoning. In the end, decisions favor the urgent over the important unless deans have well established goals and priorities (Covey, 1989).

All in all, deans face the formidable responsibility of providing instructional leadership and supervision. Increasingly, they experience complications brought on by a changing student population, a market mentality that fosters suspicion on the part of the general public, a country's prosperity driven by economics but dependent on education, and a technological evolution measured in minutes, days, and years instead of decades and centuries. The pace of the latter, at least for the moment, drives all other considerations. For deans and colleges, housed in universities conditioned by a history of slow and reactive change, taking advantage of the opportunities that such challenges provide requires changes in the mind-sets of faculty, students, the public, and deans themselves.

What Strategies Can Deans Use to Meet These Challenges?

UNIVERSITIES EXPECT DEANS to lead their colleges. To do so, deans must ensure that their colleges realize university missions for instruction and research. They must maintain fiscal stability, create environments that are conducive to carrying out the work of the college, and participate in the overall leadership of the university. In each instance, shifts in student populations, fiscal and political realities, technological advances, competing educational venues, and potential corporate demands cloud the picture of how deans might carry out these roles. Stress, ambiguity, and a realization by many that they come to the position ill equipped to carry out the tasks set before them can further dilute their ability to lead. In the complex landscape we call higher education, what does it mean to be a leader and how might academic deans fulfill this charge?

This part of the issue is divided into two primary sections, the first of which examines an overarching strategy that moves deans as managers of day-to-day operations to deans as leaders in a dynamic environment. The second part looks at strategies as they pertain to specific challenges.

An Overarching Strategy

This section highlights common views of leadership and change leadership.

Common Views of Leadership

There is no one way to define leadership and no best way to describe a successful dean: both are matters of degree. Over the past twenty years, two paradigms have dominated the scholarly work on leadership—transactional and transformational. These two rubrics derive from Burns's 1978 work, *Leadership,* in which he delineates transactional leadership as a trading of benefits between leaders and followers and transforming leadership as mobilizing others to act in a manner that is morally superior to what might otherwise be the case. Burns drew from earlier work in which scholars portrayed leadership as a complex relationship of mutual stimulation built on the characteristics, attitudes, and needs of both leaders and followers; the purpose and structure of the organization; the nature of the work; and the social, economic, and political milieu in which leaders function (Hare, Borgatta, and Bales, 1955; McGregor, 1960). Subsequent scholars stripped away the moral dimension, leaving in its place transformational leadership, the result of which is substantive change (Avolio and Bass, 1988; Bass, 1985; Bennis and Nanus, 1985; Conger and Kanungo, 1988; Peters and Waterman, 1982; Rost, 1993). Deans as leaders might fall into either of these camps.

The transactional or exchange theory of leadership posits that interactions occur between leaders and followers based on reciprocity (Bensimon, Neumann, and Birnbaum, 1989; Heifetz, 1994). As a consequence, a person's ability to lead depends on the willingness of others to be led. It is a negotiated process in which the power bases of the leader and the followers counterbalance each other (Burns, 1978). The success of such leadership endeavors revolves around a common belief that individuals can make a difference. Leaders, under this theory, tend toward the use of control and command mechanisms; organize around goals, tasks, and agendas; focus attention on the issue at hand; communicate well; match resources with the requirements of the work to be completed; and understand what motivates followers (Bensimon, Neumann, and Birnbaum, 1989; Burns, 1978; Heifetz, 1994; Hollander, 1964; Jacobs, 1970). The standard by which leadership is judged is simple: if people are influenced to engage in organizationally relevant behaviors, then leadership has occurred (Hollander, 1964). Deans who subscribe to this form of leadership tend to be authoritative.

Transformational leadership moves in a slightly different direction. Here, the purpose of the interaction is not individualistic (what's in it for me?) but

> **A person's ability to lead depends on the willingness of others to be led.**

collectively directed (how can we change our situation?) (Mintzberg, 1998; Matusak, 1997). Any power exerted by leaders and followers mutually supports a common purpose (Rost, 1993). From Burns's perspective (1978), any resulting change would need to be morally uplifting and socially beneficial. To Bass (1985), the change must be significant but not necessarily moral. For Peters and Waterman (1982), the effectiveness of such leadership depends on just how far beyond expectations followers are willing to go. Leaders in the transformational vein focus on changing the culture and disrupting the status quo. They are self-confident and directive (Bensimon, Neumann, and Birnbaum, 1989) and exhibit what Goleman (1995, 1998a, 1998b) terms "emotional intelligence." Deans who possess emotional intelligence understand themselves and their emotions, moods, and desires. They can regulate any tendency to react to impulse. They have a passion for work, an empathy for others, and the social skills needed to build rapport and find common ground. They strive to personally impact their followers by shifting responsibility to those with the greatest vested interests. They identify relevant challenges, focus people on crucial issues, and move them away from unnecessary distractions (Heifetz, 1994). And they encourage followers (or collaborators, a term Rost [1993] coined as he revised his work) to become leaders. Deans who function from the transformational view tend toward relation building and depend on shared governance more heavily than do transactional deans.

Recent literature suggests that truly successful leaders combine the two approaches. Bass (1998, p. 99) notes, "The best of leaders are both transformational and transactional but they are likely to be more transformational and less transactional than poorer leaders." The connotation here is that deans must perform the day-to-day actions of operational management but not at the expense of generating ideas and forming collective visions of the future. In so doing, effective deans make people feel significant and instill in them the notions that learning and competence matter, that people are the community, and that work is exciting (Bennis, 1999, p. 86). The ecological importance, or interrelatedness, of people, places, and ideas becomes an imperative (DePree, 1992; Helgesen, 1990, 1995; Wheatley, 1992), and the concepts of collaboration, caring, courage, intuition, and vision drive leadership efforts (Chliwniak, 1997; Regan and Brooks, 1995).

Collaboration results in connectiveness. Working in groups helps people create synergistic environments in which leaders and colleagues elicit and offer support, focus on cooperativeness and inclusiveness, and embrace shared ownership (Helgesen, 1990). Caring manifests itself in an affinity for the world and its people. It translates moral commitment into action on people's behalf. Belenky, Clinchy, Goldberger and Tarule (1986) refer to caring and connection as central to psychological development and learning, particularly for women. Leaders with courage demonstrate a capacity for moving ahead, testing ideas, and taking risks. The ability to consider equally both what is in the heart and in the mind constitutes intuition. It is a natural mental ability, strongly associated with experience. Leaders with vision can formulate and express original ideas. They enable others to think about options in new and different ways, increasing creativity, enhancing relationships, and decreasing the fear of failure (Amabile, 1998; Bass, 1998; Chliwniak, 1997; Kanter, 1997; Regan and Brooks, 1995).

Finally, the concept of shared leadership has begun to emerge. Its general premises—shared responsibility, a tangible vision, mutual influence, and a bias for action—sound suspiciously like those of transformational leadership (Bradford and Cohen, 1998). The attempt, however, seems directed at moving the concept of leadership from a person-centered to a team-based philosophy (H. Astin, 1996; H. S. Astin and Astin, 1996; Yukl, 1998). Despite agreement in theory, confusion exists as to the interpretation of the term "shared leadership." For some, it suggests a cluster of empowered leaders and followers engaging in cross-functional purposes (Ostroff, 1999). For others, it refers to the coordinated efforts of "post-heroic leadership," which make everyone in the group a leader, responsible at all levels, and collaborative in their management of the group (Bradford and Cohen, 1998; Yukl, 1998). And for still others, it signifies "teams at the top," which can vary their composition, behavior pattern, and leadership approach to optimally integrate individual, team, and nonteam performance (Katzenbach, 1998). Katzenbach (1998) makes it clear that his concept of shared leadership does not advocate for a team of leaders but rather a leadership team. He defines real teams as "a small number of people with complementary skills who are committed to common purposes, performance goals, and leadership approaches for which they hold themselves mutually accountable" (p. 217). In the end, all three models preserve the sole leader at the top of the organization. Their authors, while enamored with the notion of teams at the top, seem suspicious of human nature. Katzenbach captures their dilemma when he comments, "We create a contradiction for those in the 'leadership' role: the expectation that work would be better served by a team approach runs up against [traditional] expectations of the position. As a result, in most organizations, leadership at the top rarely functions as a team. Team performance at the top is all about doing work together, about collective action. [In such situations] real work [goes beyond] open discussion, debate, decision making, and delegation of authority" (1998, p. 111).

Bensimon and Neumann (1993) came closer to defining shared leadership outside the realm of leader-as-an-individual; they examined the concept of complex, team-centered leadership in colleges and universities. Indeed, they believe that teams dominated by solo leaders are limited in their abilities to effect and respond to change. They assert that the complex team they advocate is "more open and equalized in their conception of leadership . . . and view leadership as a shared process and a shared responsibility. . . . More effective at discerning complexity in their environments, the complex team demands shared responsibility for thinking as much as it requires shared responsibility for doing" (p. 145). Bensimon and Neumann did suggest that one person, a team builder, starts up the team, but that once the team is in place, all responsibilities are shared.

Leaders of Change

Implicit in these theories of leadership is the concept of change. Deans exist at the centers of complex relational webs comprising faculty, students, central administration, and external entities and support agencies. Their primary charge is to keep the resulting relationships finely balanced. In rare instances, balancing may mean leaving well enough alone. If faculty, chairs, staff, and students are working together for the betterment of the college and the fulfillment of its mission, then the best strategy for deans might be to support, facilitate, and get out of the way (Matczynski, Lasky, and Haberman, 1989). If, however, colleges and their faculties are victims of inertia that threatens the college's viability, deans must engage in "innovative practices" (Huffman-Joley,

1992, p. 1) that underscore their commitment to the improvement of the institution (Morris, 1981; Wisniewski, 1998). Innovative practice requires that deans become experts in how to change institutional culture—building visions of what their colleges might look like if certain prescribed changes take place and taking the initiative in planning and implementing change (Huffman-Joley, 1992).

Change agentry never simply equates to implementing the latest policy. Instead, change becomes a normal part of the work of the organization, a way of life (Fullan, 1999). Watson and Johnson (1972) describe three types of change: structure, process, and attitude. Structure change occurs when policy and procedure are modified. Process change involves alterations in the way people operate and relate to others within the institution; they include changes in communication patterns, modes of decision making and conflict management, and styles of management.

Attitude changes occur when the organizational culture is modified. Early Greeks referred to attitudinal change as *metanoia,* "fundamental shifts of mind" (Fullan, 1993, p. 3). These shifts of mind go to the heart of leading colleges and universities in today's dynamic environments. Without such shifts, deans face the task of trying to juxtapose "a continuous change theme" driven by current reform movements and calls for innovation within a fundamentally conservative education system. Without attitudinal change, the most likely outcome is status quo (Fullan, 1993, p. 3). With it, deans can "evolve the culture of the organization by building on its strengths while letting its weaknesses atrophy over time" (Schein, 1992, p. 64).

In effect, these agents of change accept, effect, implement, and regenerate organizational change (Bergquist, 1992; Guskin, 1996; Hilosky and Watwood, 1997; Keller, 1983; Mintzberg, 1989; O'Toole, 1995; Senge, 1990). Accepting change implies that deans are aware of the forces in and out of the college that exert influence on decisions made. Legislatures and the corporate sector make up external forces; administrative, student, and faculty groups exert internal pressure. In addition, deans who accept change as necessary possess the ability to shape concerns raised by college constituents into conceptual pictures of change that are organizationally purposeful. These pictures have two dimensions, telescopic and panoramic. They are telescopic in that change telegraphs organizations into the future and panoramic because the kind of change that today's leaders face cannot be piecemeal but must be comprehensive, broad, and systemwide. Together, these dimensions frame a vision, or general notion, of where an organization needs to head (Conger, 1998; Fullan, 1993; Guskin, 1994a, 1994b, 1996; O'Toole, 1995; M. Wolverton, 1998b).

The ability to read the environment and rethink the organization, however, means little if not coupled with action. Change leaders realize that organizations, and they themselves, must learn as they go. Pragmatic in nature, these change leaders continually question their assumptions and review their take on reality and the values that undergird it (Bennis, 1999; O'Toole, 1995). "Those skilled in change are appreciative of its semi-unpredictable and volatile character; and they are explicitly concerned with the pursuit of ideas and competencies for coping with and influencing more and more aspects of the process toward some desired set of ends" (Fullan, 1993, p. 12). They do not require that every minute detail of the journey be known and a plan for every contingency be in place before they begin (Carr, Hard, and Trahant, 1996; Guskin, 1996; O'Toole, 1995; Peters and Waterman, 1982). In fact, these leaders "are open to discovering new ends as the journey unfolds" (Fullan, 1993, p. 12). They simply keep change moving.

Effecting change requires that deans communicate its essence and convince others of its necessity. Leadership communication has two sides—relaying and listening. Relaying refers to communication in the more traditional sense— transmitting in an understandable way the why, what, and how of change (Conger, 1998; Cox, 1994; O'Toole, 1995). Listening involves paying attention to constituencies, gleaning not only ideas but concerns (Wisniewski, 1998). Peters and Waterman (1982) note that one of change leadership's fundamental roles is that of creating a "learning environment" where leaders and those they serve hear each other. Within such an environment, change leaders build trust and demonstrate respect for those with whom they work. Candor and honesty play important roles in determining how successful a leader is in establishing a listening environment. Even when communication is clear, forthright, and open, change causes stress. True change leaders sense the anxiety that delegating responsibility for decision making brings for those not used to taking on responsibility and for those who are not accustomed to giving it away. In effect, good change leaders are good people readers (Carr, Hard, and Trahant, 1996; Kotter, 1990; O'Toole, 1995).

Implementing change involves putting it into practice. "The most critical part of being a change agent is to generate and support ideas and possibilities" (Wisniewski, 1998, p. 51), which suggests that leaders let subordinates take credit for successes (Sherman, 1995). They think not so much about what others can or should do but about what they themselves should stop doing so others have the opportunity to contribute (O'Toole, 1995). Structurally, such inclusiveness implies shared leadership, which is interwoven into the fabric of institutional operations (Carr, Hard, and Trahant, 1996; Fullan, 1993). Operationally, change leaders understand the benefits that accrue to an organization from involving people from multiple constituencies (especially those who will later be charged with implementation) in the planning phases of the change process. With widespread participation, change goals are more likely to be held in common and resistance lessened. Change leaders believe, however, that buying in to the idea is not enough; substantive change occurs only when its processes become fully integrated into the way the organization does business—never in isolation, never as an add-on program (Carr, Hard, and Trahant, 1996; Fullan, 1993; O'Toole, 1995).

Regenerating change means starting the process over again, with new change framed by the environment and built on past changes (Hilosky and Watwood, 1997). Organizational stability becomes a key determinant of whether regenerative change takes place. Today, during periods of change where one cycle bleeds into the next, an organization that retains its leadership core from change inception to institutionalization stands less chance of becoming sidelined or derailed than do organizations that experience frequent leadership turnover (Carr, Hard, and Trahant, 1996; Cox, 1994; Guskin, 1996; O'Toole, 1995). In environments that move slowly in anticipated patterns, that forgive organizational inertia, over-reliance on custom, and a tendency to preserve the status quo, change becomes predictable and relatively easy. If one leader replaces another in midstream, little disruption occurs, and things move along very much as they have in the past. In contrast, change in a dynamic environment fraught with uncertainty becomes more radical and its consequences patently more severe. Because systemic change efforts can take ten to fifteen years and require continuity and consistency of thought and direction, change initiatives in this environment can easily disappear. For organizations like colleges and universities where deans often remain at the same institution fewer than six years (and new leadership frequently brings with it a fresh agenda and a different leadership team), systemic change usually means trouble (Guskin, 1996; Wisniewski, 1998).

Arends (1998), in describing his experience in a school of education with serious economic and structural problems, nicely sums up change leadership. First, he says, change occurs in complex human systems, and deans must start their efforts where these systems are in terms of their disposition toward change. In colleges, those systems involve faculty and staff. Second, successful change occurs when deans work with the most promising parts of a system and avoid "working up hill." They must begin with faculty and units who want improvement and who support projects that hold promise for success. Third, successful change requires good ideas, which must be communicated, prioritized, and molded into a shared vision for which faculty, staff, and administrators take collective responsibility. Fourth, successful change requires good processes of change. Deans must encourage new ways of thinking and learning and help modify organizational norms and structures that impede change. Fifth, when individual and organizational goals coincide, change occurs. Deans must understand that faculty are self-motivated to enhance their own status and sense of accomplishment. Sixth, successful change requires resources—fiscal and emotional. Inadequately supported change efforts leave a bad taste. Seventh, action pulls people in, especially if it leads to success. Small successes lay the foundation for larger ones later. Finally, change is a process that takes time.

Change places deans in the position of managing tensions between various factions of the institution while at the same time keeping the organization focused on its mission and goals.

All in all, change places deans in the position of managing tensions between various factions of the institution while at the same time keeping the organization focused on its mission and goals. When anxiety emerges from the change process, deans must absorb and contain it, maintaining "temporary stability and emotional reassurance" as the past and future of the organization are joined together (M. J. Austin, Ahearn, and English, 1997a; Lewin, 1938). Indeed, change agency involves not only acquiring new concepts and skills but also unlearning old ones that no longer serve the organization well. "Unlearning is an entirely different process, involving anxiety, defensiveness, and resistance to change" (Schein, 1991, p. 63). As change agents, deans must possess the emotional strength to support the organization as it undergoes change. The grounding for such strength lies in a true understanding of the cultural dynamics and properties of the organizational culture (Bennis, 1999; Schein, 1991).

To this point, we have suggested that deans will encounter ever more complex challenges brought on by changing demographics, a skeptical public, advancing technology, and increasingly invasive corporate demands. Further, we have argued that any mandates that result from such changes will add to, not detract from, an already full agenda—which in turn may add greater stress and lead to less effective administration.

We have also implied that if deans somehow become leaders practiced in leading change, their burdens will in some way be lightened. It may be true that deans who anticipate and confront change head on may be more effective at what they do than deans who simply sit and hope that the storm will pass.

Specific Strategies

Speaking in vague generalities about leadership offers little concrete in the way of getting the job done, however. The remainder of this section offers specific strategies that deans might employ to help move their colleges forward through today's higher education environment. The challenges deans face are multifaceted, and they must employ multiple strategies to address them. The strategies highlighted in the remainder of this section cut across all challenges:

- Create a diverse culture
- Know the legal environment

- Become technologically connected
- Strategically manage and secure financial resources
- Seek and maintain professional and personal balance
- Nurture the integrity of your college.

Each strategy captures the interconnectedness of the challenges that confront deans. For example, it makes little sense to build relevant curricula without taking into account the diversity of populations served, the role of technology-aided delivery systems, fiscal constraints, and faculty capabilities. Likewise, efforts to foster diversity in isolation from consideration of demands for accountability driven by legal and fiscal constraints seem destined to fail. In each instance, successful deans will employ all or most of these six strategies. In the case of curricular relevance, for instance, funding new delivery systems to multiple constituencies may test institutional integrity. In the case of diversity, the obvious strategies involve law, funding, and diversity itself. But balance and institutional integrity may come into play as well. If deans are to survive and flourish, they must possess the wherewithal to deal with critical issues that are reflected in these strategies.

Create a Diverse Culture

For many people, diversity refers to race/ethnicity—and primarily to white and African American because that is where some of the greatest disparities lie and where our attention has been focused (Banks, 1995; Hendley, 2000). In fact, race/ethnicity and gender loom before us as obvious forms of diversity because we can see them. So it makes sense in some ways to concentrate first on what we see. Yet concentrate as we might, we still find it difficult to accommodate, let alone celebrate, diversity (West, 1993). To complicate matters further, the definition of diversity in the United States cannot be limited to such a narrow view (Hendley, 2000). Indeed, diversity surrounds us in terms of race/ethnicity, gender, class, socioeconomic status, sexual orientation, age, ability, religion, geographic region, and so on (Cook and Sorcinelli, 1999).

Perhaps the first lesson deans learn when they tackle diversity is that "Americans believe America is whatever they [encounter] in their daily experiences" (Hendley, 2000, p. 9, quoting Oh). In some organizations, diversity means being

Latino; in others it refers to being Protestant in a Catholic university or being a woman at a military academy. Openness to diversity in American society must be fostered not only by interactions with students and faculty not like ourselves but also through institutional commitments to developing a far broader multicultural understanding than many of us presently possess (Whitt and others, 1997). In general, Americans believe that colleges and universities have a distinctive role to play in preparing people to function in a more diverse workforce (Cook and Sorcinelli, 1999). Deans can become critical catalysts in the realization of such an endeavor. To do so, they must champion the cause of diversity.

For many deans, cultivating a spirit of celebration around diversity has long been part of their work. Some have found the task at hand more difficult than they expected and see no clear way to proceed. A few have yet to begin. The task is formidable, and deans can either help their colleges take advantage of diversity or allow them to cower in its presence (Hendley, 2000). The nature of work involving diversity is often sensitive and emotional, and how a dean communicates the work to the college is as important as the work itself (Cox, 1994).

The success of any college-wide diversity effort rests on its dean's firm commitment, which is reflected through the allocation of resources, an ability to engage faculty, staff, and students collaboratively, long-range planning, and continual monitoring of progress (Cook and Sorcinelli, 1999; Gardenswartz and Rowe, 1993). The first inclination of colleges and universities is to provide access to students. When students, unaccustomed to or unprepared for the rigors of university academics, fail, the momentum shifts. We fix the students. We remediate, we begin to put academic, fiscal, and emotional support systems in place, and we experience some success. In these instances, diversity remains at the periphery—a series of programs from which funding can be siphoned when priorities change or resources become scarce (Richardson and Skinner, 1991). Moving beyond this stage requires a change in perspective: a belief that the college should and can change. It is this remaking of a college's culture around the concept of diversity that we pursue here.

Cox (1994) suggests that organizations bent on embracing diversity must ultimately change the culture, change people, change management systems, and continually educate and communicate. In the first instance, belief systems and values must be challenged. In the second, attitudes of current organizational members must be altered and selection processes for new employees revamped. In the third, policies and procedures that govern how business is conducted must be rewritten to remove institutional bias and to reward desired behaviors. In the last, discussions about group differences must be brought out into the open. Communication and education serve as mechanisms that help facilitate the three types of change.

The purpose of engaging in and maintaining open lines of communication lies in the desire to create opportunities for college members to discuss diversity, to become aware of their own attitudes about diversity, and to ascertain how those beliefs affect students and colleagues (Cook and Sorcinelli, 1999). Education is most commonly deployed as the initial foray into organizational change around diversity. When people have the opportunity to explore diversity-related material where both their beliefs and knowledge about diversity are acknowledged and addressed, their level of understanding is enhanced (Tatum, 1992). Without a thorough understanding grounded in research, however, educational efforts may miss the mark (Cox, 1994). A considerable base of knowledge and expertise is available to those who facilitate educational programs. Educational efforts could backfire if facilitators do not take advantage of such resources. A further shortcoming of traditional diversity education lies in its delivery. Often these opportunities for education are limited to one group and are no more than one-time awareness training seminars (Stage and Manning, 1992).

Instead, college members need multiple avenues into the dialogue. For instance, deans can advocate and provide the resources for workshops; intensive, year-long seminars; new faculty and staff orientation; and specialized forms of training, such as sensitivity and awareness building, for those who work closely with students. Readings and annotated bibliographies can be compiled; Web pages can be designed around the topic; and ways for people to share ideas, concerns, and information on an ongoing basis, such as brown bag lunches and electronic message groups, can be created (Cook and Sorcinelli, 1999).

Of the four strategies that Cox mentions, changing the culture constitutes the greatest challenge. Redefining a college's culture requires a mutual reshaping of individuals and the organization in which they function over time (Gardenswartz and Rowe, 1993) Deans can begin by assessing the current state of the college: its history, policies, and procedures as they pertain to diversity, psychological climate, and behaviors of people within it (Gardenswartz and Rowe, 1993; Hurtado, Milem, Clayton-Pedersen, and Allen, 1999). To collect data, specific instruments can be designed to assess the organizational culture and analyze the attitudes and perceptions of faculty, staff, and students. For example, colleges can undertake the development of an employment opportunity profile. This form of organizational audit examines minority participation across the organization in terms of numbers and placement in the power hierarchy. In other words, what types of representation do various groups have within a college, and what positions do they hold? Are women concentrated in staff positions? Do the majority of faculty of color hold the assistant rank without tenure? Are disabled populations represented at all? (Cox, 1994; Gardenswartz and Rowe, 1993).

Next, deans can build a base of need: why is diversity important to the college? Two strategies are important here. One revolves around the definition of diversity and the other on how conversations about diversity are framed. In the first instance, deans must set broad parameters around the concept of diversity but focus on issues the campus and college communities consider important. Most widely accepted definitions of diversity refer to any physical, cultural, social, economic, and philosophical characteristics that might affect teaching and learning (Cook and Sorcinelli, 1999). For a historically black institution, the desire might be to attract highly qualified white students and faculty to provide diversity in thought and action.

In the second, deans can suggest how diversity furthers the overarching goals of the academy, which can be accomplished in a couple of different ways. First, deans can point to the larger charge that universities face—that of shaping the attitudes of the country's future leaders (Hurtado, Milem, Clayton-Pedersen, and Allen, 1999). Second, the conversation can be focused on good teaching and learning, not just on diversity. By doing so, deans can demonstrate how all students benefit when their colleges' core values revolve around inclusiveness, attention to multiple perspectives, and mutual respect (Cook and Sorcinelli, 1999).

Changing people is almost as difficult as changing the culture. The easiest way to go about it is to recruit and hire new people who value diversity. Efforts to increase the participation in colleges of faculty from underrepresented groups will involve actively pursuing qualified candidates who bring diverse perspectives. As a first step, deans must ensure that similar perspectives are represented on selection committees (Toma and Palm, 1999). The old adage rings true, even in colleges. We gravitate toward those who are most like us (Stage and Manning, 1992). In colleges and universities, this approach is also the most unrealistic because positions rarely become available. Revitalizing a college solely by using this technique could take years, if not decades.

The most feasible method of tackling this charge involves working with the people already in the college. Deans begin by speaking with sensitivity, awareness, and honesty about the college's efforts to increase diversity. They build support by talking to faculty and staff about a redefinition of college priorities to include diversity. They serve as role models. They draw faculty in by asking them to share what they believe to be problems and possible solutions (Cook and Sorcinelli, 1999).

As deans pursue the goals of diversity, they must start with those who are committed and interested but not limit the choice of program and planning participation to those who are comfortable with diversity. Deans who do so end up preaching to the choir. Instead, work groups must be diverse to the greatest degree possible across age, gender, race/ethnicity, discipline, rank, and so forth. In addition, deans can invite a few highly respected faculty to participate, even if they show little initial inclination toward involvement. Sometimes an educative program that requires representativeness as a criterion for selecting participants can serve as a mechanism for working these reluctant but visible people into the process. Similar approaches provide a means for including otherwise marginalized populations as well. Finally, deans must model collaboration around issues of diversity. For instance, cosponsoring programs and events with other colleges or units sends a clear message to college constituents that diversity matters and that working with others helps the college reach its goals (Cook and Sorcinelli, 1999; Gardenswartz and Rowe, 1993).

Changing the organizational systems that are in place requires that the college take a hard look at the way it operates. In creating an environment that supports a diverse work force and diverse perspectives, organizations must ensure that members of all cultural backgrounds can contribute and reach their potential without running up against institutional or social barriers (such as environments in which differences are treated as a weakness; lonely and non supportive work environments for nontraditional faculty, staff, students, and administrators; lack of organizational savvy; or greater comfort in dealing with one's own kind) (Cox, 1994; Morrison, 1992). Cox (1994) distinguished between formal structural barriers, such as power distribution, promotion policies, and decision-making procedures; informal obstacles, such as networking, informal communication, and mentoring systems; and institutional bias, such as a reliance on self-promotion, a desire to compartmentalize work, and monolingualism.

Before beginning to address systems issues, a college's mission statement must explicitly address diversity. Committee structures within the college must reflect diversity (Gardenswartz and Rowe, 1993). Every effort must be made to eliminate exclusionary practices that overtly or subtly keep people from becoming fully participating college members. At the same time, deans must protect against tokenism. Often, colleges have few women or persons of color, for example, and in attempts to be inclusive, these few individuals end up appointed to all the committees. As such, their opinions can be summarily dismissed as not representative of the whole. In addition, the added burden of being the visible minority places them in jeopardy when it comes to making progress toward tenure or promotion unless conscious efforts are made to recognize their contributions to the college (Cox, 1994).

Every effort must be made to eliminate exclusionary practices that overtly or subtly keep people from becoming fully participating college members. At the same time, deans must protect against tokenism.

Deans also must be cognizant of the needs of faculty in the classroom, where their belief in diversity, or lack thereof, plays out. Lectures and rote memorization commonly used in classrooms have their bases in Eurocentric ways of thinking, processing information, and learning (Katz, 1989; Stage and Manning, 1992). They may be modes of learning unfamiliar to the increasing number of ethnic and racial minorities on today's college campuses, however. In addition, a Eurocentric bias can manifest itself in course content in three ways: overt prejudice, unrealistic perspectives, and lack of inclusiveness (Stage and Manning, 1992). The continued persistence of these biases proves a disadvantage to those who have the ability to do well yet do not share Eurocentric cultural values. Addressing the concerns of classroom materials, however taboo, will be critical to a dean's success in managing diversity.

Helping faculty to become aware of the assumptions they make about how learning occurs and how these assumptions can disenfranchise a growing number of students is a beginning. Deans can sponsor workshops on alternative ways of learning and teaching strategies that are more inclusive and use a variety of formats to present the material and evaluate students. By broadening a faculty's repertoire of teaching techniques, the learning experiences of students from all cultural backgrounds will improve (Stage and Manning, 1992). In addition, faculty need the tools to manage classroom dynamics around diversity and to change classroom practices and curriculum content to enrich the learning experience of students (Hurtado, Milem, Clayton-Pedersen, and Allen, 1999). These tools and programs must focus on building personal awareness of stereotyping, prejudice, and bias, and the value of diversity. The goal in the classroom must be to promote mutual respect, appreciation of differences, and value of common bonds (Promising Practices Team, 1999). The fulfillment of such a goal requires that faculty understand how, and have the ability, to create a safe environment in which students and faculty can explore strategies that empower them as change agents (Tatum, 1992).

Finally, deans must engage in ongoing evaluation and monitoring of efforts to achieve diversity to determine their effectiveness (Gardenswartz and Rowe, 1993). The original data collected to gain an understanding of the culture and climate of the college can serve as baseline information against which deans and their colleges can measure their progress (Cox, 1994). Another possible tool derives from a 1999 report released by the Presidential Initiative on Race, which highlights the characteristics that promising practices for racial reconciliation had in common. The framework developed can be adapted easily to all types of diversity and provides a set of benchmarks against which deans can assess their colleges' efforts to increase diversity. These include promoting inclusive collaboration, educating individuals about diversity, raising consciousness about diversity, encouraging participants' introspection, expanding opportunity and access for individuals, fostering civic engagement, affecting systemic change, and assessing the impact of efforts on the community served (Promising Practices Team, 1999). Appendix A provides further examples of diversity-related strategies that deans might employ.

Know the Legal Environment

Kaplin and Lee (1995, p. 4) comment that today "the law reaches too far and speaks too loudly. . . . Legal proceedings and compliance with legal requirements are too costly. . . . They divert higher education from its primary mission of teaching and scholarship; and they erode the integrity of campus decision making. . . . " While deans are not expected to be legal experts, they should possess a grasp of commonly litigated issues to determine when to seek counsel (Kaplin and Lee, 1995; Toma and Palm, 1999). Legal issues that surround discriminatory student admissions and faculty hiring, tenure, and promotion practices are perhaps the most pervasive legal concerns deans face. Cases dealing with academic freedom and students' expectations in terms of program quality also devolve to colleges. Attending to the legalities of these issues helps deans and colleges meet the letter of the law. Instilling a culture of ethical practice meets its spirit. Indeed, "law floats in a sea of ethics" (Covrig, 2000, p. 41). Appendix B provides deans with a list of available resources specific to these areas.

Antidiscrimination in Practice. Admissions procedures, hiring and promotion decisions, search and selection processes, and conduct or misconduct on the job are governed by the U.S. Constitution, federal and state statutes, and administrative rules and regulations (Toma and Palm, 1999). For deans, the greatest challenges lie with rules and regulations that pertain to affirmative action, equal opportunity, and disabilities legislation. Affirmative action refers to government-sanctioned efforts to benefit persons in legally protected classes to compensate for past discrimination (Kaplin and Lee, 1995; Pratt, 1999; Watkins, 1999). Pertinent legislation includes Title VII (42 U.S.C. §2000e *et seq*.), which prohibits discrimination in employment; Title VI

(42 U.S.C. §2000d *et seq.*), which prohibits discrimination based on race; Title IX (20 U.S.C. §1681 *et seq.*), which prohibits discrimination based on sex; and the Fourteenth Amendment, which provides equal protection (Kaplin and Lee, 1995). Equal opportunity regulations seek to prohibit discrimination against people in these classes. Disability legislation deals with environmental access and climate (Schatzberg, 1999).

A landmark case, *Regents of the University of California* v. *Bakke,* 438 U.S. 265 (1978), allowed higher education institutions to establish affirmative action programs "so long as those programs promoted a compelling state interest" (Pratt, 1999, p. 451). The ability to give some consideration to race in university admissions procedures stems directly from this ruling (Pratt, 1999).

Currently, however, arguments against these programs reflect one of two attitudes: either they are discriminatory against nonbeneficiaries, or they stigmatize intended beneficiaries (Watkins, 1999). Programs, in whole or in part, have recently been eliminated, either by the courts or by the will of the people. If deans are to successfully come to terms with the ramifications of current movements to dismantle public policy, they can begin by educating themselves about pertinent court decisions. With this end in mind, we briefly summarize two seminal cases and two state referenda as a start.

The concept of affirmative action in higher education was first successfully challenged in 1994 in a case brought by a Hispanic student against the University of Maryland at College Park (*Podberesky* v. *Kirwan,* 38 F.3d 147 (4th Cir., 1994)). Podberesky sued the university, alleging denial of equal protection under the Fourteenth Amendment, when he was ruled ineligible for a scholarship offered exclusively to African Americans. Although the university argued that it provided the scholarship to remedy the effects of past discrimination against African Americans, the 4th Circuit Court of Appeals found otherwise and struck down the program. The court stated that what the university cited as effects of past discrimination were not causally related to past discrimination at the university (*Podberesky,* pp. 154–161) but the result of societal discrimination. Further, it found that the program resembled "outright racial balancing [more] than a tailored remedy program" (*Podberesky,* p. 160).

In 1996, the 5th Circuit Court of Appeals handed down a second important ruling. Contrary to the Supreme Court's ruling in *Bakke,* it found that diversity in education does not serve a compelling state interest (*Hopwood* v. *Texas,* 78 F.3d 932 (5th Cir. 1996), *cert. denied,* 116 S.Ct. 2581)). In this case, Hopwood and three other white applicants sued after being denied admission to the University of Texas School of Law, citing violation of the Fourteenth Amendment of the U.S. Constitution and Title VI of the Civil Rights Act of 1964. The 5th Circuit, like the 4th Circuit, sought a causal connection between the law school as a past discriminator and its present activities with regard to minority students but found no proof that one existed (*Hopwood,* pp. 951–955). The court suggested that a preferential system for the under-privileged without regard to race would be constitutional (Wightman, 1997).

These findings do not necessarily hold true for other appellate court juris-dictions. Indeed, the 1st Circuit Court of Appeals in 1998 acknowledged that *Bakke* was "still good law and, . . . under some circumstances, diversity might be a sufficient compelling reason to justify race-conscious actions" (*Wessman* v. *Gittens,* 160 F.3d 790 (1998)).

State ballot initiatives have abolished affirmative action programs in higher education in California and Washington. Washington's Initiative 200, passed in 1998, prohibits the state (including its public colleges and universities) from "discriminating against or granting preferential treatment to individuals or groups based on race, sex, color, ethnicity or national origin" (Pratt, 1999, p. 460). California's Proposition 209, an earlier version of the Washington ref-erendum, passed in 1996. In subsequent litigation, the 9th Circuit Court of Appeals found that Proposition 209 did not violate the Equal Protection Clause and was not preempted by Title VII.

In contrast, equal opportunity regulations appear to excite less resistance. These regulations (along with affirmative action policies) provide guidance for hiring, interviewing, and other placement practices of administrators and faculty alike. Recent court decisions about affirmative action do not affect protections against discrimination that equal opportunity regulations pro-vide. Employment decisions based only on individual qualifications and merit alleviate concerns of discriminatory employment practices (Watkins, 1999). Any violation of these statutes requires that universities present sufficient evi-dence of a legitimate nondiscriminatory reason behind the action (Kaplin and Lee, 1995).

Colleges invest time and resources in the people they hire. Mistakes can prove costly, especially when those denied employment deem the hiring process unfair and seek legal remedies. Deans can create proper hiring cultures where those responsible for conducting interviews are aware of appropriate or inappropriate questions to ask during interviews. Questions about marital status, future family plans, national origin, health, age, or religious practices all can be construed as biasing the potential employer around classifications protected under antidiscriminatory acts. Clarifying these questions for faculty and staff helps to send the message that hiring practices are based on career-related qualifications (Toma and Palm, 1999).

Deans can create proper hiring cultures where those responsible for conducting interviews are aware of appropriate or inappropriate questions to ask during interviews.

Issues of faculty tenure, promotion, and dismissal lie at the core of college administrative work. A negative decision can undo a faculty member's career or disrupt a college for years (Leap, 1995). Typically, decisions to grant or deny tenure are based on flexible criteria, such as scholarly credentials and budgetary, economic, staffing, and related nonacademic concerns (McHugh, 1973). Often no tenure formula exists that poses acceptable levels of quality or quantity of an applicant's research, teaching, service, or collegiality. Such flexibility provides colleges with a great deal of latitude but opens them up to possible litigation when tenure or promotion is denied and the criteria undergirding the decision have no firm basis in written protocols (Leap, 1995).

Even though courts seem reluctant to reverse the administrative evaluations of faculty and in fact have held that institutions need not provide reasons for denying tenure except when a protected class or fundamental right is involved (Leap, 1995; Paretsky, 1993; Toma and Palm, 1999), deans may want to avoid judicial interference on actions taken within a college. In these instances, seeking counsel before taking any adverse personnel action is wise. Additionally, using regular performance evaluations and posttenure reviews give deans a record that can be used to support positive personnel actions, such as promotion, as well as negative actions, such as discipline or termination. Finally, structuring decision-making committees in ways that do not favor one group over another can ameliorate the possibility of bias in promotion as well as hiring decisions (Toma and Palm, 1999).

A further consideration that confronts deans, both in student admissions and employee hiring and promotion, stems from legislation concerning persons with physical disabilities. Section 504 of the Vocational Rehabilitation Act of 1973 and, more recently, the Americans with Disabilities Act require institutions receiving federal funding to provide reasonable accommodations for persons with disabilities (Schatzberg, 1999). Although physical access may remain the responsibility of the university, environmental concerns fall to deans.

Many educational institutions fail to provide environmental climates in which all members feel comfortable, safe, and valued. Ism-neutral programs that inculcate beliefs and habits where organizational members celebrate people regardless of race, gender, or ability (to name a few) may offer real alternatives to preferential programs (Cantú-Weber, 1999). Moves to initiate such options will not only improve college work environments but will possibly help deans forestall future litigation against their colleges.

Sexual Harassment. Sexual harassment, another form of discrimination, is among the most common complaints deans encounter (Rossbacher, 1999). Referred to as "the hidden campus violence," harassment is pervasive in higher education. Current estimates of the number of college students sexually harassed by professors approximate 50 percent (Dziech and Hawkins, 1998, p. x). (This figure does not take into account unacceptable actions of those in supervisory roles who deal with university employees.) In colleges and universities, sexual harassment is clearly prohibited as a form of sexual discrimination under Title IX of the 1972 Education Amendments and, where employees are concerned, under Title VII of the 1964 Civil Rights Act (Paludi, 1990; Riggs, Murrell, and Cutting, 1993). In many instances, however, "the policies and procedures in place to enlighten and inform the individuals about sexual harassment are not enough" (Paludi and Barickman, 1998, p. 32). Part of the problem lies in the lack of understanding that surrounds the issue, not only for faculty and students, but among deans as well. Most recognize that sexual harassment has to do with the distribution of power, but many remain unclear as to exactly what constitutes this type of behavior (Paludi and Barickman, 1998). For deans, building a vocabulary that captures the nuances of sexual harassment provides a platform from which they can initiate discussions that raise college-wide consciousness.

No universally accepted definition of sexual harassment exists (Dziech and Hawkins, 1998; Paludi, 1996; Riggs, Murrell, and Cutting, 1993), although the legal definition of it comprises two types: *quid pro quo* (something for something) and hostile environment (Paludi, 1996; Watts, 1996). *Quid pro quo* sexual harassment is exemplified by sexual negotiation: sexual requests rewarded for compliance or punished for failure to comply. Hostile environment sexual harassment refers to "an atmosphere that is created in the college . . . that is perceived by an individual to be hostile, offensive, and intimidating" (Paludi, 1990, p. 4). A broad spectrum of acts falls under the umbrella of sexual harassment (Riggs, Murrell, and Cutting, 1993). To help deans differentiate degree, Fitzgerald (1996) delineates five subcategories based on the severity of the act. *Gender harassment* comprises generalized sexist behavior and remarks intended to insult, degrade, or convey sexist attitudes (generally about women); it is usually not intended to elicit sexual cooperation. *Seductive behavior* is defined by sexual advances that are unwanted, inappropriate, and offensive. *Sexual bribery* occurs when reward is promised following solicitation of sexual activity or other sex-linked behavior. A threat of punishment by sexual solicitation is the next level of *sexual coercion*. Finally, *sexual imposition* constitutes a gross sexual imposition, assault, and/or rape.

Besides raising awareness of and sensitivity to harassment, deans can continually critique the institutional factors that pose potential risks or foster sexual harassment. And they can examine policies, procedures, and educational and counseling efforts in place that address issues of harassment (Paludi and Barickman, 1998; Riggs, Murrell, and Cutting, 1993).

On a final note, sexual harassment is assumed to be a women's issue. While it is largely true that awareness and understanding of the issue came to light as women entered the workforce, the incidence of men as victims of this type of harassment has also increased. A climate that permits such harassment of men by women or by other men jockeying for power and position damages the college as a whole (Dziech and Hawkins, 1998).

Academic Freedom. Within the faculty culture, issues of conduct and performance are often supported or challenged based on the principle of academic freedom. Even when we separate misconduct concerning inappropriate sexual activity or unethical amorous relationships, constitutional issues around the First Amendment and academic freedom are tricky. The rationale for academic freedom revolves around "preserving and encouraging the robust exchange of ideas within a community of scholars" (Toma and Palm, 1999, p. 60). In a landmark case, *Sweezy* v. *New Hampshire* (1957), the U.S. Supreme Court's decision identified academic freedom as the university's right to determine for itself on academic grounds who may teach, what may be taught, how it shall be taught, and who may be admitted to study (Doughtrey, 1991). The dilemma facing deans in cases that hinge on a clear understanding of academic freedom is that none exists. Universities, courts, and individuals often interpret the concept differently.

The disparity lies in educators' perception of academic freedom as it relates to "custom and practice," while those in the legal system define it according to the "rights and responsibilities" of the teaching profession (Kaplin and Lee, 1995). Indeed, in *Piarowski* v. *Illinois Community College*, 759 F.2d 625 (7th Cir., 1985), the court appreciated this tension between faculty prerogatives and institutions' rights, stating that the term "'academic freedom' . . . is equivocal. It is used to denote both the freedom of the academy to pursue its ends without interference from the government . . . and the freedom of the individual teacher (or in some versions—indeed in most cases—the student) to pursue his ends without interference from the academy" (p. 629).

Issues of academic freedom lie in the realm of constitutional law and contract law, and deans and other administrators must be able to make the distinction (Kaplin and Lee, 1995; Toma and Palm, 1999). In public institutions, for example, deans find they are limited "by both contract law and constitutional concepts . . . and perhaps also by state statutes or administrative regulations . . . " (Kaplin and Lee, 1995, p. 300). Despite the seemingly overwhelming protections afforded by these laws and regulations, "courts have not specifically held that a distinct right to academic freedom exists" (Olswang and Fantel, 1980). Indeed, in some instances, courts defer to the judgment of the decision makers (schools/universities), in effect leaving the determination of how academic freedom is exercised to them (Strope, 1999).

When deans act on a case, they can alleviate some of the uncertainty by clarifying several crucial points. First, deans can determine whether the issue is an individual or institutional concern. Second, they can decide whether the interest of the individual in engaging in an activity outweighs the interest of the college in preventing it. Third, deans can answer the question of whether the college would have taken adverse action against the faculty member even without the activity being involved. Fourth, they can evaluate the situation in terms of how the activity in question affects the college's ability to maintain effective working relationships and provide education (Toma and Palm, 1999). Discovering the potential impact on the college helps deans determine whether to pursue legal counsel.

Contractual Relationship with Faculty. An issue similar to academic freedom that deans must confront is the tension that exists today between the professionalization and bureaucratization of the faculty. In 1914, the American Association of University Professors (AAUP) was organized for the benefit of the nation's professoriate; with professionalism as its goal, issues of academic freedom, tenure, governance, and pay came within its purview (Hutcheson, 2000).

Bureaucratization of the academy has been inevitable, however, despite the AAUP's goal of professionalism. Indeed, with its work now involving collective bargaining, that organization has shifted its objectives toward the preservation of the "material conditions of the profession, conditions that recognized professors as employees" (Hutcheson, 2000, p. 2). Thus, faculty must continue to function within the "bureaucratized nature of the university" (p. 185). And in response at least in part to faculty unionization, higher education began using more part-time faculty, developed and increased the use of post-tenure review, and moved toward greater dependence on computer technology.

Hutcheson (2000) suggests that while scaling back publication and service requirements may make nontenurable positions attractive to some, the residual responses of others could be damning for deans and their colleges. For instance, the tenured and tenure-track faculty professors at Eastern Michigan University went on strike in 2000 over the issue of part and full-time lecturers, alleging that eliminating tenure-track positions by hiring temporary lecturers "undermined tenure and academic freedom" (Leatherman, 2000, p. A16). Although the parties reached a tentative settlement of their dispute, the issue of faculty unionization increasingly opens a festering wound for deans and the academy.

The issue of faculty unionization increasingly opens a festering wound for deans and the academy.

Contractual Relationship with Students. During the years when in loco parentis was the norm, the relationship between universities and students was viewed as comparable to the relationship between children and parents and protected in the same manner. Indeed, universities were charged with the rights, duties, and responsibilities of parents in supervising students. With the protest movements of the 1960s, however, colleges and universities moved away from this doctrine, and subsequently the relationship between students and institutions became an implied contractual agreement (Kaplin and Lee, 1995).

"Students are now considered consumers of higher education, as opposed to wards of institutions" (Toma and Palm, 1999, p. 86). As such, they enter into contracts with universities (and more specifically with colleges, departments, and programs) through actual signed matriculation agreements or implied contracts by virtue of tuition payment. In exchange for their tuition, institutions agree to provide academic programs and services that will help students reach their academic goals. Programs, services, and practices outlined in departmental catalogs, handbooks, and brochures set the parameters of these contracts.

Toma and Palm (1999) cite contractual issues (personnel matters, student complaints) "among the most common legal issues that deans . . . confront" (p. 5). Deans have an obligation to ensure that their colleges provide the promised programs and services. If students deem programs unsatisfactory, deans may be mandated by the courts to rectify the situation, should complaints be filed for failure to perform contracted services. Reviewing programs and program delivery systems regularly helps colleges maintain academic integrity. Keeping faculty, staff, and students in compliance with both written and spoken "promises" avoids potential legal concerns while maintaining the integrity of the college.

Ethical Practice. Colleges can be viewed as professional organizations, or at least as organizations of professionals—groups of highly trained individuals who work as scholars conducting research and teaching students. As such, it might be assumed that colleges are communities that expect their members to conduct themselves in a certain way and find certain other ways unacceptable (M. L. Wolverton and Wolverton, 1999). In effect, over time colleges did establish implied codes of conduct based on established habits, which evolved into patterns of practice (Camic, 1992). Much of American society functions with this understanding of ethical principles, where acceptable behavior minimizes conflict and allows people to work together effectively (Kerr, 1994).

Universities have enjoyed a great deal of autonomy, in part because they were trusted to govern themselves in this ethical manner (Boyer, 1996; Kerr, 1994; Wilcox and Ebbs, 1992). The problem with academia's unstated rules of conduct lies in the growing suspicion by the general public that, at best, they draw lines in the sand over which college members fear to tread (Garcia, 1994). And at worst, they "immunize institutional practices against criticism" (Putnam, 1995, p. 268). An emerging perception is that universities and their colleges have allowed themselves and their members to slip away from their ethical principles.

Indeed, Swazey, Lewis, and Anderson (1994), in a survey of 2,000 faculty and 2,000 doctoral students, found that 22 percent of the faculty knew colleagues who misrepresented data, 33 percent knew of inappropriate authorship credit, and 40 percent knew colleagues who misused university resources. Surprisingly, 50 percent of the graduate students would not report unethical behavior on the part of a faculty member out of fear of retaliation, and 65 percent of the faculty shared a similar fear. And while 94 percent of the faculty agreed that institutions should monitor unethical practices, only 13 percent believed that any regulatory action actually occurs.

Such unethical behavior touches all cornerstones of the academy: the nature of relationships between faculty and students, academic freedom, and research (Cheney, 1993; Gewirth, 1990; Penslar, 1995; Soley, 1995; Wagner DeCew, 1990). Each impinges on the other. For instance, most agree that the best professors care for their students beyond the classroom and are not only available but also accessible to them (A. W. Astin, 1993). The ethical considerations around platonic student/faculty relationships, to say nothing of amorous ones or cases of outright sexual harassment, manifest themselves in accusations of favoritism and biased evaluation of students' performance (N. A. Davis, 1990; Markie, 1990).

Likewise, a potential quagmire exists for deans as they strive to protect the academic freedom of faculty and students while at the same time ensuring an educational environment free from discrimination (Gewirth, 1990; Wagner DeCew, 1990). Any activity on the part of deans to regulate what goes on in the classroom, what research is carried out, and which texts get used is viewed as a threat to this fundamental premise. Yet the same expression of freedom can give birth to an environment that stifles or offends special populations of students and faculty and thus denies them the very academic freedom deans attempt to protect (Wagner DeCew, 1990).

In a similar vein, because the underlying premise of research in higher education is the quest for truth, charges of fraud, deception, misconduct, and misrepresentation become all the more alarming (Cheney, 1993; Penslar, 1995; Soley, 1995). Growing public skepticism about scientific misconduct and mistrust in the institution's ability to regulate itself has generated watchdog agencies that seek to maintain ethical standards in research (Hallum and Hadley, 1993). The conflict of interest between "pure" research and research funded by industry fuels concerns that distorted motives drive research results and what is reported (Korn, 1993). Even so, with the current publish or perish environment, abuses of authorship and manipulation of data leave the scientific community questioning the appropriate response (Caelleigh, 1993; Mangan, 2000; Woolf, 1993). Such ambivalence "allows unethical behavior to go undetected, and . . . unpunished" (Whicker and Kronenfeld, 1994, p. 9) and places deans in the role of monitoring faculty and student research.

Universities are still looked upon as leaders in society, but without a commitment to acting on sound ethical beliefs, universities stand to slip farther from their hallowed precipices (Bennis and Nanus, 1985; Burns, 1978; J. W. Gardner, 1990; Komives, Lucas, and McMahon, 1998; Kouzes and Posner, 1993, 1995). Deans, as agents of their institutions, can take precautionary stances in an effort to prevent misbehavior and potential harm to students, faculty, and the university. Deans, as leaders, must set the ethical tone (Wilcox and Ebbs, 1992).

Robert Hutchins once remarked that the "chief test of the administrator was more of character than of intellect" (Bogue, 1994, p. 6). Yet a cursory reading of the *Chronicle of Higher Education* suggests that some deans suffer "from a poverty of ideals. . . . We read of the most surprising, disappointing, and occasionally bizarre leadership behavior of . . . deans . . . placing their clients and colleagues, their organizations and institutions, in harm's way" (Bogue, 1994, p. xii). Some of these incidents were perpetrated by truly unscrupulous deans. Others occurred as the result of poor decision making when deans failed to search deeply for the answers to questions such as who am I? who are we as a college? who is the university? (Bardaracco, 1998). The answers to such questions undergird credibility and a willingness on the part of others to trust those in leadership positions (Conger, 1998; Kouzes and Posner, 1993). In the end, deans have a social obligation to serve as models of ethical and wise leadership. Personal ethics are a bedrock of good deaning. Wise leadership involves personal integrity, which stretches beyond a commitment to life-shaping principles to being true to one's self (Cashman, 1999; Covey, 1992; Josephson and Hanson, 1998).

Deans can move their colleges beyond an awareness of the law to ethical practice by entering into a dialogue with faculty and students about what constitutes acceptable behavior.

Clearly, the ethical character of colleges and universities can only be supported and cultivated when reinforced by everyone (Wilcox and Ebbs, 1992). Deans can move their colleges beyond an awareness of the law to ethical practice by entering into a dialogue with faculty and students about what constitutes acceptable behavior.

Become Technologically Connected

If deans head colleges that possess unlimited resources, they can add new technologies and upgrade old ones at will. If resources (human and fiscal) are finite, however, deans must approach technology issues from a different perspective. In essence, they must answer three questions: How can this college use technology to enhance students' learning and the delivery of education? What is the most effective use of technology as it relates to the productivity of personnel? And what is the most fiscally efficient use of technology?

Enhancing Student Learning and Education Delivery. Technology offers the opportunity for a pedagogical shift from teacher-initiated instruction, where the instructor is the center of knowledge, to student-focused instruction, where computer-based curricula force students to struggle with multiple sources of information and take control of their own learning (Batson and Bass, 1996). Used effectively, technology supports commonly agreed-upon principles of good practice in undergraduate education (Chickering and Ehrmann, 1996; Chickering and Gamson, 1987).

For instance, the use of technologies, such as electronic mail, creates the opportunity to increase student/faculty contact. Students can ask questions and easily receive feedback on work. Asynchronous delivery via Web sites allows students to review materials at their convenience. Participation of diverse students becomes more equitable and widespread when on-line discussions ensue (Chickering and Ehrmann, 1996; K. C. Green, 1997). In addition, the use of computers and the Internet can encourage collaborative problem solving and information processing (Batson and Bass, 1996). It also provides the tools and resources for active learning. Time-delayed or real-time conversations and computer-generated simulations let students play out theories and test hypotheses in an applied mode of learning (Batson and Bass, 1996). Because they enjoy working on computers, students tend to spend more time on task and to strive to meet higher expectations (Chickering and Ehrmann, 1996). And perhaps most important, technology can accommodate a variety of learning styles. Literacy for today's youth involves not only text but also image and screen (Brown, 2000).

Despite such optimism, skepticism abounds as to the efficacy of technology-based learning (D. P. Jones, 1995). The concern is that such endeavors fall short of expectations because colleges rush to keep up with cutting-edge instructional technologies without demand for the service, organizational infrastructure, or curricular content (K. C. Green, 1997). The issue raised is whether students in these learning situations receive an education comparable to other degree-granting programs (Connolly, 1994; Johnstone and Krauth, 1996). Merisotis and Phipps (1999) contend that the very notion of access to college in the distance-learning context is unclear. And they insist that the human factor cannot be ignored or replaced in higher education. In fact, they suggest that research shows that technology is not as important as factors such as learning tasks, characteristics of learners, students' motivation, and the instructor. At the very least, failure to ground the content of a curriculum in principles of good practice generates courses taught electronically but not necessarily quality education (Johnstone and Krauth, 1996).

Deans can make the entire process of distance education and on-line course development proceed smoothly and purposefully by continuing to ask fundamental questions about need and feasibility and by observing environmental trends that shape the future (Gilbert, 1996; Massy and Wilger, 1998). In essence, they must plan for the integration of technology into teaching and learning. To begin with, deans can ask staff to build a profile of the existing technology structure in their colleges and determine how technology is currently used (Sink and Jackson, 2000).

While a baseline of information about the college technology infrastructure is being established, deans can engage their colleges in identifying academic goals, key activities to help achieve those goals, and the appropriate use of technology to carry out required activities (Ehrmann, 2000). For instance, one goal might revolve around ensuring that all graduates, whether they attended college on campus or at a distance, can work well in teams. Collaborative learning provides an example of one activity needed to reach this goal, and the appropriate technology might be some form of on-line communication.

Engaging in such an endeavor requires deans not only to keep abreast of technological advances but also to understand the ways that students learn

(Van Dusen, 1997). For example, deans who experiment with on-line simulation exercises, discussion lists, and chat rooms gain an appreciation for how students process information (Batson and Bass, 1996). By doing so, they can inform and help evaluate the reasonableness of technology choices. The final aspect of planning is assessment. Deans must periodically revisit college goals as they relate to technology and its application in the teaching and learning environment.

Personnel Productivity. The introduction of technology into the classroom, either as a means of enhancing course instruction or as a mode of providing access to courses, takes the form of campus-developed telecourses or Web-based learning modules. When faculty view technology-based instruction as a movement toward making their presence irrelevant (Batson and Bass, 1996), colleges experience poor buy-in, scattered efforts, and a lack of coherence that limits intended educational outcomes (Ehrmann, 1994).

For those eager to engage in technology-based instruction, the learning curve can be steep and technological neophytes can become frustrated by limited or uneven access to equipment, software, and support; the lack of information on good integrative practices; and a misunderstanding or ignorance of the legal use of intellectual property. They may inadvertently deemphasize teaching and learning in their attempts to use technology to enhance it, and they may focus on isolated, individual student development in lieu of group participation when constructing course materials (Gilbert, 1996; Van Dusen, 1997). The result may be a stagnant syllabus posted on line, a mediocre video of a professor lecturing, or a poorly conceived teleconference (Batson and Bass, 1996; K. C. Green, 1997).

Deans can foster cohesive technological integration by developing flexible guidelines that encourage faculty engagement within the fiscal means of the college. They can facilitate group learning among colleagues through workshops on Web page design, the use of Power Point, and interactive discussion groups. Deans can also eliminate some glitches by hiring qualified staff to service computers and manage networks (Van Dusen, 1997). They can put support services in place by employing students as assistants. If Web page designers who can be loaned to faculty are part of the college personnel structure, then faculty may decide to participate in such endeavors (Gilbert, 1996). These support services become paramount for faculty with heavy teaching loads or research agendas. Because of time constraints, faculty who might otherwise be willing may choose not to pursue technology integration.

As the infusion of technology into colleges expands, constraints imposed by intellectual property laws become contentious and can serve as disincentives for faculty. Some refer to the situation as higher education's "ticking time bomb" (Gorman, 1998; M. M. Scott, 1998; Welsh, 2000). In the face of dwindling resources, concerns about who owns the intellectual property created by faculty, who controls it, and who is compensated for such property loom large for administrators. These are uncharted waters for colleges and their deans, and in some instances, state governing boards of higher education have stepped into the fray. For example, the Kansas Board of Regents developed strict ownership policies for their technology-based systems (Welsh, 2000). As more faculty invest time and energy into developing technical applications, deans must be able to articulate faculty and college intellectual property rights.

Efficient Use of Fiscal Resources. Deans commonly encounter four options in instructional technology Web courses, Web-centric courses, Web-enhanced courses, and descriptive Web sites. One hundred percent of the instruction in Web courses occurs through computer technology. These courses are available anywhere, anytime over the Internet. Web-centric courses base 50 percent of their instruction on the Internet; the remainder takes place in regularly scheduled classroom meetings. Web-enhanced courses resemble campus-based courses but make significant use of the Internet, including Web sites. About 25 percent of instruction is handled through technology. Descriptive Web sites provide college, programmatic, and faculty information. They are usually points of information dissemination used, in large part, for marketing purposes (Boettcher, 2000).

Development and support costs can include but are not limited to supplemental pay for faculty, work/study wages for students to help develop computer programs, graduate students to help with the transformation, curriculum design specialists and technology support staff, hardware for faculty, computer labs for students, networks, servers, and software for statistical analysis, spreadsheet configuration, graphics, simulations, database management, and data presentation (K. C. Green, 1996).

Estimates suggest that to develop a typical classroom-bound, forty-five-contact hour, three-credit Web course can run as high as 1,440 hours and $72,000 in faculty time and dollars alone. Web-centric courses that convert twenty-three lecture hours range in cost from $5,750 to $26,450, and Web-enhanced courses cost from $2,750 to $12,650. When support staff and operating costs such as equipment, copyrights, software licensures, and overhead are considered, the total average costs jump to $184,000 (100 percent Web based), $74,000 (50 percent Web based), and $20,000 (25 percent Web based) (Boettcher, 2000, pp. 191–197).

Technology costs are substantial and, we hazard a guess, never fully comprehended by colleges or their deans. In trying to manage the costs of instructional technology, deans face three realities. One, costs of instruction will increase when technology is used to supplement existing activities or as add-ons to current courses. Two, the development and use of instructional technology will inevitably require new expenditures to acquire those technologies; cost savings, if any, will come from other activities, such as future course delivery. Three, instructional technology is better suited for some types of courses than others (for instance, seminars do not lend themselves to this format as well as large lecture-style courses do). In short, deans will not be able to manage costs without revisiting both instructional practices in their colleges as a whole and current budgeting practices (Kaludis and Stine, 2000).

First efforts are often funded through temporary sources, such as foundations, technology firms, or institutional grants, and they often end in failure because no sustainable funding materializes. Data suggest that only 43 percent of the nation's two- and four-year colleges have strategic plans for how technology will be used in instruction, and fewer than 30 percent have financial plans for ongoing support, replacement, and software updates (K. C. Green, 1996, 1997). Inadequate financial planning, both for start-up costs and long-term maintenance, is an indicator that a dean or a college does not fully understand the arena in which they are experimenting (Johnstone and Krauth, 1996).

Colleges must live within their means, and deans must help them prioritize how they spend money. "A starting point for academic communities is to identify critical issues and to consider how computer networks will be incorporated into their [colleges] in order to . . . develop and adopt policies regarding the appropriate use of computers and networks" (Connolly, 1994, p. 41). Once priorities are set, budgets need to reflect them. Because technology has become a part of the academic experience, systematic increases in spending for technology should be part of any college's financial plan.

For the next few decades, deans will have to bridge the gap between paper-based and electronic environments (Metz, 1995). "The difference between the experience of technology as a guiding light and technology as a pool of quicksand ultimately depends on an institutional and programmatic vision, a strategy, and a plan. These three components are neither easy nor quick; but each is clearly essential" (K. C. Green, 1997, p. 6). Gladieux and Swail (1999, p. 9) offer the following prescriptions for deans and colleges: place access at the core of the system design; keep the promise of technology in perspective; learn from the distance learning pioneers, and do not repeat their mistakes. See Appendix C for a list of resources on technology and higher education.

Strategically Manage and Secure Financial Resources
Two elements of funding that relate to a college's well-being loom large for deans. The first has to do with fiscal management, the second with the procurement of resources. Indeed, a dean's success, at least in part, is measured "in terms of [his/her] ability to gain additional resources for the college and to restrain departmental desires so as to arrive at an overall reasonable budget request" (Meisinger, 1994, p. 51). Since 1977, total higher education expenditures have more than doubled (Bowen, 1977; Honeyman and Bruhn, 1996). One consequence of this growth in spending has been increased public scrutiny and in response the development of complex accounting systems and procedures in universities and colleges (Vandament, 1989).

Fiscal Management. The expansive scope of financial management activities in which deans engage ranges from the "development of major strategic plans to the conscientious collection of minor fees from students" (Vandament, 1989, p. 2). The first step in dealing with these responsibilities lies in recognizing the enormity of the task at hand. Primary financial responsibilities for deans reside at two levels: consequential and important but incidental. The first group includes assessing college revenue needs, making allocation decisions, establishing expenditure targets and strategies for the college, and retaining and developing good faculty and staff through salaries and other types of fiscal support. It also entails evaluating financial planning and adjusting college budgets based on changing conditions and perceived future needs, controlling fraud and mismanagement, and searching for more cost-effective ways of delivering services (Vandament, 1989).

In addition, some deans have been required (or sought on their own volition) to expand their colleges' revenue bases by pursuing contract research, engaging in patent and laboratory development and management, and in establishing or participating in research parks. Such activities generate an added resource of revenue, indirect cost recovery, that deans must also manage. These responsibilities demand an added degree of fiscal sophistication on the part of deans if they are not handled by central administration (E. C. Phillips, Morrell, and Chronister, 1996). Deans can delegate many of these consequential fiscal tasks to business managers but must be cognizant of the underlying concepts that drive financial decisions in the college. Deans are ultimately responsible for their colleges' well-being.

Incidental duties can be assigned to nonacademic support staff trained to carry them out within the constraints of set college or university procedures. They include evaluating and adjusting programs and college processes to reduce waste, ordering general building repairs, maintaining appropriate supply levels, and providing timely income and expenditure information to departments and programs (Vandament, 1989).

The second step in rising to the growing fiscal management demands placed on deans requires that they build their general understanding of finance and budgeting. A budget is a plan written in financial terms, the development of which begins with a college's mission, goals, and objectives, not its current year's budget (Haimann and Hilgert, 1987; McBride, 2000; Meisinger, 1994). Used strategically, budgets serve as mechanisms for setting college priorities that communicate a plan of action. Used judicially, they serve as systems of control and political statements of intent—contracts with college constituencies (Meisinger, 1994).

For most deans, mastering the intricacies of operating budgets proves challenging and matching revenues with expenses an illusive exercise in futility. All unrestricted income, including indirect cost recovery from grants and funded research, that is regularly available to a college for instructional activities and departmental support falls within the purview of the operating budget. It also includes any restricted funds, such as endowed positions and sponsored programs. Through budget planning, income gets allocated to cover basic departmental and college expenses, such as personnel and day-to-day operating costs. Ancillary activities (for instance, summer programs) that are financially self-contained because they derive income directly from students or the public either generate separate budgets or are considered distinct operating budget items. Unlike capital budgeting for building projects, in which deans engage on occasion, operational budgeting remains an almost constant irritant. Deans find themselves working up the budget, working over the budget, or struggling to cut the budget midyear.

> **Deans find themselves working up the budget, working over the budget, or struggling to cut the budget midyear.**

Three fundamental concerns govern all budget decisions—the degree to which expenditures improve programs, the impact of activities funded through the budget on workload, and the extent to which the mission of the college is expanded, diminished, or redirected by budget expenditures (Meisinger, 1994). For deans, typical issues involving expenditures include teaching loads; course credit weighting factors; distribution of faculty ranks, salaries, and sabbaticals; use of part-time faculty and graduate assistants; support staff, general support, and operating outlays; and the funding of technology. Each issue raises its own set of questions. For instance, how does program or college accreditation impact teaching loads and class size? What is the distribution of faculty by rank across programs? Do salaries serve as incentives or disincentives? What ratio of full-to part-time faculty maximizes the viability of college programs? Which departments are support-staff poor? Which are rich? Do operating expenditures for travel, telephone, and supplies meet the needs of college personnel? To what extent could the use of technology reduce faculty and support staff load and cut the college's personnel needs? At what costs? (Meisinger, 1994).

This final potential budget expenditure deserves greater attention. For deans, it represents the greatest number of unknowns. Because the life cycle of most equipment and software is extremely short and their costs illusive, deans face the challenge of making good decisions about instructional and information technology expenditures. The use of instructional technology at the college level should fulfill at least one of three purposes: expand access, enhance quality, or cut costs (Pumerantz and Frances, 2000). For instance, most colleges use Web-based information centers as a mechanism to save costs because they allow for relatively high college visibility at a reasonably low cost. The problem lies in current fiscal practice. Technology-based courses get developed because it sounds like a good idea or because everyone else is doing it. Little attention is paid to how much such endeavors really cost. But costs are important. In general, the estimated cost of developing a fully stand-alone three-credit course runs from $100,000 to $400,000, depending on the selected media and the existing computer infrastructure (Boettcher, 2000, pp. 191–197). In allowing these types of practices to exist, deans try to manage expenditures instead of costs, which is analogous to shutting the barn door after the horse is out. Instead, by managing costs, deans can determine whether to make expenditures and if so, how fast and for which technologies (Kaludis and Stine, 2000).

Critics of the academy believe that short-term, professional development courses may not adequately provide the fiscal expertise that deans need (McBride, 2000; Townsend and Bassoppo-Moyo, 1996). They suggest instead that higher education doctoral programs offer and require courses in budget and finance and higher education law that deans might audit. Deans can also keep abreast of these issues by consulting resources such as the *Chronicle of Higher Education* for information on public finance debates in the United States, fiscal issues with respect to higher education, and legislative policies.

In addition, several rather straightforward strategies regularly employed can help deans maneuver their colleges through the budget melee:

- *Learn how your university's finance office operates.* Where do individual colleges fit within the university budget process? How much flexibility do colleges have? Is the central budgeting office in the habit of asking for midyear budget paybacks?

- *Know where college resources come from and what drives the amount received.* For instance, does enrollment determine university allocations to the college? If so, what is the college's target population? Has it changed? Should it be expanded? How will target expansion impact pool quality?
- *Know what the money can be used for.* Are funds restricted to particular research projects and programs, or can they be appropriated for general operating and instructional expenses?
- *Be fiscally conservative.* Do not spend money the college does not have.
- *Pay attention to over- and underexpenditures.* Determine why expenses do not match expectations.
- *Open up the process (provide access and information and seek input), especially when budgets are tight.* Faculty and staff may not like what happens, but they may find living with it easier if they understand why controversial decisions were made.
- *Reduce fixed costs to provide greater flexibility by examining how support staff are used and by evaluating the teaching balance among full-time faculty by rank, adjuncts, and graduate assistants.*
- *Determine where and in what ways technology best serves the college.*
- *Have a technology plan.*
- *Evaluate programs longitudinally in terms of centrality to college mission and direction, program uniqueness, enrollment demands, quality, and cost.* Pay attention to how increases or decreases in program capacity or demand impact other programs.
- *Consider contingencies.* Plan for revenue shortfalls, unexpected expenditures, and the effective use of unexpected excess revenues and savings. Make sure any unbudgeted funds are used for high college priorities, not impulse purchases that do not further the college's goals.
- *Create a reserve by withholding a small portion of funds to use as a buffer against budgetary uncertainty.* Such funds can provide a safety net that keeps useful activities going until permanent funding sources are identified.
- *Broker college resources to provide focus.* For instance, provide release time to work on initiatives and funds for conference attendance; invest in making change happen (McBride, 2000; Meisinger, 1994; Vandament, 1989).

Resource Procurement. Resource procurement refers to soliciting unearned gifts or engaging in revenue-generating activities that lie outside the normal purview of colleges (Brittingham and Pezzullo, 1990; Carbone, 1987; Elliott, 1995). Universities and colleges have always accepted donations from grateful alumni. Some have long histories of actively seeking out such contributions to supplement university coffers (Carbone, 1987). But as the costs of providing higher education outpaced government spending and income generated by tuition and fees, fundraising became one of the key means of expanding college and university revenues (E. C. Phillips, Morrell, and Chronister, 1996). Indeed, "development activities . . . have grown to be a major part of administrative work at most educational institutions . . . [and] there is a trend toward assigning specific fundraising responsibilities to deans" (M. R. Hall, 1993, p. 1).

The problem for deans is that they have little or no experience or knowledge of how successful development efforts should occur (M. R. Hall, 1993), nor do they possess the professional training typically associated with such work (Townsend and Bassoppo-Moyo, 1996; Vandament, 1989). To complicate matters further, many deans simply do not like chasing dollars. They take rejection personally and, if truth be told, avoid the task as often as possible (Gitlow, 1995).

To help remedy this situation, deans must see fundraising for what it is: a search for funds to help colleges achieve worthy goals (Gitlow, 1995). M. R. Hall (1993) provides a framework that deans might use in formalizing college fundraising processes. First, deans must define the vision for the future of development activities in the college and devise a plan for bringing it to fruition. Second, they must build an organizational infrastructure to accommodate such work. This task can be accomplished by building a circle of advocates and identifying potential business, foundation, and individual donors. A conflict sometimes arises at this point between deans and their universities' development officers. Both groups seek private support from external sources but for different purposes. Deans want funds and endowments to go directly to their colleges; university development officers attempt to extract larger gifts that can be shared across the university. This approach sometimes restricts a college's potential donor pool. Another major component of this infrastructure must focus on issues of stewardship, such as record keeping and gift management. Deans must ensure that gifts are used as their donors intended, and they must convey this assurance to the donors (Brittingham and Pezzullo, 1990; Carbone, 1987; Elliott, 1995).

Third, one of the best ways to garner financial commitments from potential donors is to involve them in the work of the college. Some enjoy meeting and dealing with deans. In their eyes, deans are their colleges. Others prefer serving on advisory boards. Still others expect to interact directly with students and faculty or actively engage in college/community projects. All prospective donors must be selected carefully so that donors' interests match the college's objectives. Fourth, deans must set goals in terms of dollars and what the college plans to do with the money once it is received. Fifth, deans must solicit donations. And such donations should stretch donors financially. Giving when it hurts a little not only breeds a vested interest in the college but also helps colleges avoid accepting gifts that are inadequate for their designated purposes. Finally, deans have a fiduciary responsibility to donors. They must ensure that monies are well spent and that each philanthropic investment yields the anticipated return, whether it is an investment in the here and now (such as equipment) or in the future (scholarships, perhaps) (Brittingham and Pezzullo, 1990; Carbone, 1987; Elliott, 1995; Gitlow, 1995; M. R. Hall, 1993).

Today, deans often hire development officers who specialize in this type of work (Kelly, 1991; G. T. Smith, 1977). Because integrity is central to long-term success in development work, deans who employ development staff must make certain that these officers adhere to acceptable practice (M. R. Hall, 1993). A related fiduciary responsibility that befalls deans has to do with determining the cost effectiveness of the development staff. In other words, does the staff generate more dollars than are spent on salaries and operating expenses? (Meisinger, 1994).

A second major source of revenue for research universities arrived with the passage of the Bayh-Dole Act in 1980. The act allows universities to enter into partnerships with pharmaceutical, retail, mining, computer, engineering, and other for-profit entities to fund research. In addition, universities can now patent research results and earn royalties from licensing their inventions to companies in the United States (Press and Washburn, 2000; U.S. General Accounting Office, 1998). The effect of Bayh-Dole on universities has been mixed. On the one hand, it has fostered a collaboration between universities and industry, which has yielded some very important new products (for example, anti-AIDS treatment, genetically engineered crops, hypertension, and cancer drugs). In these relationships, "the research or invention is usually provided by the university, while the mechanism of commercialization is provided by private industry" (Faris, 1998, p. 1). On the other hand, commercial forces increasingly determine university fiscal and programming priorities. Most universities operate technology licensing offices to manage their patent portfolios, often guarding their intellectual property as aggressively as any business would. Schools with limited budgets pour money into commercially oriented fields of research while downsizing humanities departments and curbing expenditures on teaching (Press and Washburn, 2000).

As deans consider the financial benefits of engaging in such partnerships, they can help their colleges safeguard against possible infringements on academic freedom by limiting contract restrictions placed on their colleges. They can mitigate adverse, long-term repercussions for the university by considering how profits can benefit not only their own departments but others across campus. Appendix D provides a list of resources that examine finance, budgeting, and fundraising issues.

Seek and Maintain Professional and Personal Balance

Establishing balance is an issue of time. All deans have the same amount of time to divvy up among competing priorities. And we assume they do so judiciously and wisely. That, indeed, deans have their acts together—at work, at home, and in life. That they can prioritize tasks important to their jobs and those crucial to their personal well-being. And that somehow they strike a balance that satisfies both sets of needs. In truth, demands on time consume and control many deans. They struggle with whether to lead a college or engage in scholarly activities. Whether to remain loyal to the faculty camp or fully entrenched in the administrative one. Whether to deal with the immediate or long-term consequences of current crises and situations. Whether to have a personal life or a professional one (Gmelch, Wolverton, Wolverton, and Sarros, 1999; Lindberg, 1995). To some extent, deans can take control of their agendas by managing time and stress better, by planning and prioritizing, and by seeking personal and professional balance.

Time and Stress Management. Learning how to use time effectively can go a long way toward easing the strain that can engulf the deanship (Oncken and Wass, 1974; Oncken, Wass, and Covey, 1999). The first step a dean needs to take is to figure out what he/she does by conducting a time audit. Simply keep track at fifteen-minute intervals of how time is spent. Do it for a day, then expand the time intervals to an hour and continue recording work and personal activities for a week, perhaps even a month. During this exercise, deans should also attempt to gain an understanding of when during the day, week, or month they perform at their peak, when they concentrate best, and when they have the fewest distractions (Drucker, 1967). Once deans establish what they do and when they do it most proficiently, they need to examine the self-imposed expectations under which they function. Budgeting every second leaves little time for the unexpected. Working harder does not necessarily improve time management, but it does wear deans out faster. Deans must continually ask themselves what the best use of their time is. The answer might be that it is time to quit trying to do everything (Drucker, 1967; Lewis, Garcia, and Jobs, 1990; Oncken and Wass, 1974; Oncken, Wass, and Covey, 1999).

> **Working harder does not necessarily improve time management, but it does wear deans out faster.**

Nuisances get in the way of best intentions. Deans can determine how they spend time, try to eliminate waste, and focus on what is important, but phones ring, people "pop in" with just "one question," mail arrives, and clutter builds up. Deans can manage phone and electronic mail more efficiently by responding to it less often. For instance, they can return calls when at least two items need to be discussed rather than addressing each concern individually. In addition, they can respond to messages twice daily, choosing times when they are least productive. As to interruptions, deans can make them as short as possible by greeting interrupters at the door and carrying on discussions in the corridor. In the office, deans can signal that the encounter should be brief by standing when speaking with interrupters. Finally, deans can be preemptive by following Henry Ford's example. When asked why he dropped in on other people so often, he responded that it was easier for him to leave their offices than it was to get them out of his. Clutter, the last but perhaps most debilitating nuisance in terms of time management, derives from a culturally imposed axiom: if it is written down, it must be important. Searching through stacks of paper wastes time and adds stress. What is the worst thing that will happen if I throw this away? is one of the best questions deans can ask themselves (Cottrell and Layton, 2000).

Most important, delegate, relegate, subjugate: the secret to adding meaning to deans' work lives is to do more of the things that they enjoy and delegate more of those they do not. Deans cannot give away all tasks they do not want to do, but by delegating a significant number of them, they will have more time to do those things that matter. Professionally and personally, deans should do things that add meaning and quality to their lives (Mintzberg, 1998; Oncken and Wass, 1974; Oncken, Wass, and Covey, 1999; R. A. Scott, 1993). Finally, flexibility helps. Simple things like recognizing that some events can be controlled and some cannot and setting personal and subordinate deadlines lend order, and order conserves time and helps reduce stress (Gmelch and Miskin, 1993; Ivancevich and Matteson, 1987; Monat and Lazarus, 1977; Schuler, 1984). Deans also need to remember that mentoring and networking are not just for beginners. Everyone needs a sounding board and a safe place to vent his/her frustrations (Nies and Wolverton, 2000).

Boundary Management. Boundary management at work is a matter of planning and prioritizing for the college. It begins with a vision about what the college is and what it wants to be, a set of long- and short-term goals that serve as guides to help the college reach that vision, and a clear understanding of where the dean fits into the overall scheme of bringing the vision to fruition. This task sounds simple but indeed is quite difficult. Deans must remember that it is a college's vision; a dean alone cannot accomplish it. In addition, goals must be prioritized as to urgency and importance. Mark Twain once said, "I've suffered a great many catastrophes in my life—most of which never happened." Deans who fail to distinguish between the urgent and the truly important fall into Twain's trap.

Experts suggest that, under normal circumstances, effective deans spend 20 to 25 percent of their time on issues that are both urgent and important and 15 percent on troublesome areas that may have a sense of urgency but are not particularly important. The truly efficient dean spends less than 1 percent on nuisance problems that are neither important nor urgent. Attending to prioritized goals, then, consumes a large proportion of an effective dean's time. Finally, deans can write down the steps and determine what needs doing by the week, the month, and the year. They should not expand the boundaries; they can redefine them if necessary but only after reassessing and adjusting priorities (Covey, 1989).

Balance. Boundary management at home is a matter of finding balance. Begin by listing personal and professional priorities, combine these lists, and prioritize them again. These priorities emanate from a vision of who the dean is personally, as a family member, and as a professional. It culminates in determining what it means to have an optimal experience as a dean. Deans who attempt to stay involved in research sometimes forget to set priorities that include research as part of their professional agenda. Under such a scenario, research and writing eat into whatever personal life they have because their boundaries are too permeable or simply do not exist. To gain balance in their professional lives, deans must set aside time for scholarly projects (and perhaps establish a research team to help accomplish some of the research) or make a conscious choice to forgo research efforts.

For most, establishing balance ultimately hinges on whether they can learn to work more efficiently. Conflicts between work and personal priorities will arise, but deans can use them to identify inefficiencies in work (Coughlan, 1994; Friedman, Christensen, and DeGroot, 1998; Grace, 1982). Effective deans realize that an enriched personal life makes for a more productive dean (Friedman, Christensen, and DeGroot, 1998; Prock, 1983). Striking a work-life balance can lead to more satisfying personal lives and efficiency in work processes (Friedman, Christensen, and DeGroot, 1998). Clarity in professional and personal purpose, recognition and support of the whole person (personal and professional), and experimenting with the way work is done are three ways to alleviate the conflict between work and personal priorities (Friedman, Christensen, and DeGroot, 1998).

How seductive it is to feel needed, to be crucial, to be praised, to know what you do is important. For many self-driven deans, the slightest institutional

> By succumbing to the wishes and desires of others, deans unwittingly sacrifice their own personal integrity and wonder why their very full lives seem somehow incomplete.

prodding may push them into a perpetual state of disequilibrium. By succumbing to the wishes and desires of others, deans unwittingly sacrifice their own personal integrity and wonder why their very full lives seem somehow incomplete.

Nurture the Integrity of Your College

Institutional integrity has to do with how the general public perceives its colleges and universities. It hinges on the success universities have in building alliances with people and organizations in a fashion that fulfills recognizable public needs. Throughout the post–World War II period and well into the 1980s, universities maintained public trust primarily because of two major thrusts— one to open up access to higher education, the other to build a world-leading research establishment. Since then, however, public priorities have shifted and the perception has been that colleges and universities have not responded to these new public needs (Bok, 1992; Cole, 1993; Winston, 1994). Indeed, Helen Astin (in Albert, 1994, p. 8) suggests that rising concerns about "quality, accountability, and productivity are simply ways of asking higher education: are you still with us?"

As a whole, it appears that the American public believes that colleges and universities should be engaging in collaborative efforts with communities and other public and private entities to tackle current social ills, such as K–12 education, health care, and the environment (Albert, 1994). And while faculty conduct research in these areas, the tie to practice sometimes seems remote. An even bigger issue may lie in public sentiment about undergraduate education. Two primary constituents—parents who send their children to college and businesses that hire them once they have finished—hold fairly succinct notions of what it is that colleges should be, but are not, doing. Students, they believe, do not graduate from college as mature, independent thinkers with good work habits. And they do not, for the most part, exhibit ethical and moral stamina (Bok, 1992; Marchese, 1994). Constituents blame these workforce issues in part on a shift in college priorities away from teaching and toward research (Bok, 1992; Krahenbuhl, 1998). The simple remedy to many is to redirect faculty effort toward teaching and away from research. Such a perspective misses the point, however; what is taught is not as important as what is learned and how that knowledge is put to use (Boyer Commission, 1998; Carnegie Foundation, 1990; Krahenbuhl, 1998; Ramaley, 2000).

Deans play a critical leadership role in reclaiming the public trust (Krahenbuhl, 1998). Several approaches to this endeavor lie within their purview—redefining faculty work, reframing academic departments, refocusing department chairs, reconnecting colleges with communities, and revisiting the concept of change leadership.

Redefining Faculty Work. Universities and their colleges create faculty positions to meet the needs of the institution. As needs change, so must faculty work (Batson and Bass, 1996; Ehrmann, 1994). We sometimes lose sight of this fact. Deans who view faculty as fixed assets believe that they are unable to help their colleges respond to changes in institutional priorities. They see faculty as protected by the mantle of academic freedom and in many respects beyond administrative control. Deans who function within this paradigm seldom ask faculty who are no longer active researchers to teach more or engage in service activities and, if they do, may not reward such behavior. As a consequence, these faculty become trapped in a system that belittles their efforts and offers no prospect of advancement. In the end, many take out their frustrations on students, which in turn reflects poorly on the institution and erodes public trust (Krahenbuhl, 1998).

Deans who shift paradigms view faculty as variable assets. These deans understand that faculty interests differ over time. They design workload systems where participants agree on yearly responsibilities that make sense for the college and challenge faculty to remain engaged in fulfilling institutional needs (Krahenbuhl, 1998). In theory, this system works—but only as well as its evaluation counterpart is fair and thorough. North (1995) suggests that when it comes to teaching, many colleges suffer from the Lake Wobegon effect, where all faculty exhibit above-average teaching abilities. She contends that colleges should not depend solely on student evaluations to determine teaching effectiveness. She advocates adding unannounced peer reviews and self-reviews as they relate to the other two types of assessment. No matter what the system of assessment, evaluation and rewards must reflect the progress made toward fulfilling the agreed-upon responsibilities (Krahenbuhl, 1998).

In addition, adequate support for faculty retooling must be in place. Faculty may need to develop, improve, or change pedagogical skills or update course content to incorporate information technology (Alstete, 2000). For example, deans can provide travel grants for participation in training programs in active learning, summer grants or release time for developing new content, in-house workshops in classroom assessment, and consultive peer intervention for those faculty with specific classroom performance problems (M. Wolverton, 1998a). Besides fiscal resources, deans can send an explicit message that teaching counts by discussing it all the time, sending letters of encouragement and praise to faculty, and dropping in on class sessions (North, 1995). If institutional integrity, at least in part, hinges on classroom interactions between faculty and students, then deans can further this cause by redefining faculty productivity. Implementing a program of development and improvement of the college's faculty that underscores the needs of the individuals and the institution is one means of doing so (Alstete, 2000).

Reframing Academic Departments. Regaining or building public confidence requires that academic departments perform effectively in terms of educating students and interfacing with the communities they serve, and efficiently in terms of using resources. In a fast-paced environment, meeting these expectations falls to those organizations that can be responsive, innovative, and entrepreneurial. Agile units can restructure on demand for optimal efficiency by adding or eliminating positions. They share resources across common functions and are headed by highly trained administrators. Such requirements suggest a unit that is the antithesis of the academic department. In the case of typical academic departments, unit size varies, membership within units is fairly stable, and they are for the most part self-contained. As a consequence, small departments do the same amount of bureaucratic business as larger ones but do so less efficiently. Rarely do deans eliminate faculty lines or programs; instead, they starve them to death. In addition, most departments limit their leadership pool to current faculty members, who rotate in and out of the chair position with minimal training and many times with little interest (Edwards, 1999).

Because there is little turnover and a great deal of autonomy, traditionally configured academic departments are unusually effective points of resistance to upper administrative calls for change. For deans bent on improving public perception, the challenges are great and the solutions evasive, but they do exist. Deans can, for instance, do away with departments and in their stead form college faculties, program committees, or larger integrated divisions. Such moves might work especially well in small colleges or in situations where the direction on campus is toward interdisciplinary research and teaching. A second option lies in redefining department responsibilities, pushing all business and personnel decisions (other than hiring, tenure, and promotion) to more central locations. A third alternative might be to work within the current structure (Edwards, 1999). In this instance, deans work to change the academic culture of departments, using evaluation as the means of change. In effect, the notion is to build on a more flexible understanding of faculty work within departments as it pertains to institutional integrity. Annual unit evaluations help department chairs negotiate faculty work assignments in ways that maximize what is accomplished collectively by the faculty. In doing so, chairs can ensure that institutional needs are addressed and that each faculty member has a full complement of activities in support of the institutional mission (Krahenbuhl, 1998). Deans can reinforce the importance of this goal by using report card systems as guides in determining salary adjustments. The mere existence of a report card creates social pressure on departments to give greater attention to the core meaning of the institution (M. Wolverton, Gmelch, and Sorenson, 1998).

Refocusing Department Chairs. Department chairs fulfill many roles. Some are faculty related, such as recruitment, selection, and evaluation. Others are managerial in nature and have to do with daily departmental oversight. Still others revolve around the chair as a scholar. Without a doubt, however, the most elusive role, leadership, often gets summarily ignored (Bensimon, Neumann, and Birnbaum, 1989; Gmelch and Miskin, 1995; Keller, 1983; Tucker and Bryan, 1988). Many surmise that this situation has occurred because chairs come to the position without leadership training, without prior administrative experience, without a clear understanding of the complexity of the role, and sometimes with a sense of duty but little enthusiasm for the job (M Wolverton, Wolverton, and Gmelch, 1999). They are not prepared or equipped to deal with increasing legal and organizational demands, and they harbor only vague notions of what it means to be entrepreneurial and responsive (Albert, 1994). As a result, they misconstrue leadership to mean management and in doing so immerse themselves in a process of maintenance rather than one based on creativity and innovation.

Many universities do invest in training for department chairs, but too often the training remains sporadic and narrowly focused on fiscal and reporting responsibilities. The obvious solution is to strengthen the preparation for leadership through more consistent development opportunities. Doing so might include ongoing seminars where chairs across campus interact with each other. It could include sending chairs to workshops and conferences that focus on chair-leadership (Edwards, 1999).

But it could mean reframing the structure of the position. Under this scenario, deans help chairs delineate between the work that must be done within the department and work that can be done for the department. Deans can also strengthen the competencies of the support staff assigned to a department through selection, evaluation, and training. Large departments may run more efficiently with an assistant to the chair, an associate chair, or a department coordinator to carry part of the daily workload. If administrative offices expand, deans work with chairs to partition work efficiently (McAdams, 1997).

Finally, in some colleges, faculty become chairs because it is their turn or because no one else will do it. Deans might eliminate some issues of institutional integrity by examining the process of selecting chairs. Giving greater authority to chairs who are ambivalent about their administrative commitment and/or are ill prepared for the task will likely end in lackluster leadership that instills mistrust rather than confidence in college constituencies.

Reconnecting with the Community. It seems foolhardy at best to believe that colleges can build meaningful connections with their communities by focusing on one aspect of academic life, say service, at the expense of the other two, research and teaching. To do so seems synonymous with trying to fly a plane missing one wing (teaching) and an engine (research). Instead, colleges must strive for integration across research, teaching, and service (Krahenbuhl, 1998). Indeed, the goal must be the development of a mutual sense of stewardship and responsibility toward and in concert with the community (Ehrlich, 2000; Krahenbuhl, 1998).

In the short run, deans can hold their colleges accountable to their various communities by providing a report of sorts. For example, the Rossier School of Education at the University of Southern California experimented with what it terms an academic scorecard. College members began with the market indicators used by *U.S. News and World Report* and added indicators that responded to central administration's concerns about the quality of faculty, students, and programs and the school's operational efficiency. They suggest that colleges must examine what they do from four perspectives: academic management, internal business, stakeholders, and innovation and learning. Each perspective relates to one or more communities that colleges serve. For each one, faculty within a college set goals and determine financial and operational measures and targets. For example, under academic management, one goal might be to improve budget performance. Its measures might include net surpluses of income from endowments and indirect cost recovery, and its target might be to increase this surplus by 5 percent over the next two years. A goal from the perspective of stakeholders might be to measure and improve alumni/employer satisfaction, and one from the internal business perspective might deal with fulfilling agreed-upon obligations to the local community. Finally, from the perspective of innovation and learning, colleges could examine increases in student learning or the impact of service-learning on the communities served (O'Neil, Bensimon, Diamond, and Moore, 1999).

Building awareness of the contributions that colleges make to their communities, region, and nation provides a beginning upon which deans and their colleges can build. In 1916, John Dewey argued that the survival of American democracy requires civic engagement and that education is the key to such engagement. Over time, we have lost (or perhaps never fully had) this sense of civic connectedness between higher education and the community. Some blame this disjuncture on the general breakdown of society (Putnam, 1995);

others point more specifically to the pervasiveness of research in colleges and universities and its impact on undergraduate education and community service (Boyer, 1990b; Boyer and Mitgang, 1996; Zamson, 2000). No matter what the cause, Dewey's cure still remains viable: higher education must engage in its civic responsibility to society (Carnegie Foundation, 1990; Ehrlich, 2000; Ramaley, 2000).

This is a tall order, which some colleges and universities have taken to heart. The evidence of these efforts lies in the proliferation of service-learning and campus-community partnerships. Such endeavors must be well thought out and conspicuously interfaced with a college's mission. If not, colleges run the risk of failure because resources become overtaxed and communities and faculty become partnered out (Ramaley, 2000). The result is more community disillusionment with higher education.

Using colleges of architecture as examples, Boyer and Mitgang, in *Building Community* (1996), suggest strategies for reconnecting colleges and communities: building an enriched mission, emphasizing diversity with dignity, setting standards based on learning goals but without standardization, designing a connected curriculum that is flexible, liberal, and integrated, creating an inclusive climate for learning, developing a more unified profession that joins academic and professional communities together, and pursuing this in service to the nation. In following such strategies, deans can lead their colleges in preparing competent graduates who appreciate the necessity of carrying out their work in a manner that attends to human needs and the environment. The upshot of this framework for institutional renewal is a higher education experience that prepares people for work in, and with, communities (Mitgang, 1996).

Revisiting Change Leadership. Deans serious about changing their colleges must educate themselves about the concept of change. They must signal that change is valued, create an environment conducive to change, and understand how people respond to change. The first step toward rebuilding institutional integrity rests entirely with deans. They must determine where their goals lie and once they have done that, their actions must reflect their beliefs. For instance, if a dean decides that the way to build public trust is by improving classroom teaching, then he/she must demonstrate to faculty that teaching is indeed important. Saying that teaching counts and then putting most of the resources and emphasis behind research undercuts any attempts to improve teaching. Deans must ask themselves how their intentions are perceived. North (1995) suggests deans can assess what others believe about a dean's commitment by using a simple two by two matrix called the Johari Window. The four quadrants are I know/they know; I know/they don't know; I don't know/they know; and I don't know/they don't know. Appendix F provides both an image and description of the window.

Deans serious about changing their colleges must educate themselves about the concept of change.

Second, deans must create a climate in which change can flourish. To do so, they must provide adequate resources; encourage involvement by faculty, administrators, and staff; and tie efforts to guidelines for promotion, tenure, and rewards (Singleton, Burack, and Hirsch, 1997; M. Wolverton, 1998b). They can offer real support by providing office space, student assistants, release time, seed money, and clerical support (Singleton, Burack, and Hirsch, 1997).

Finally, people respond differently to the prospect of change. Some embrace it, some dabble in it, others wait and see, and a few openly oppose it. Ramaley (2000) categorizes these four groups as committed, cautious, skeptical, and resistant. She suggests that three distinct barriers separate the groups. The divide between the committed and the cautious derives from discipline-based definitions of research and scholarship. For instance, change-cautious faculty might ask whether teaching reflects true scholarship. The tendency in any change effort is to lean too heavily on the committed faction and burn them out. Instead, deans must expand their base of support by drawing in cautious faculty. To do so, they can provide clear signs, in terms of financial resources and rewards, of what it is they value. Skeptics see no reason to change because they perceive no clear evidence that new ways work better. They might say, "We have always sorted faculty using publication and grant-generation records; how would rewarding teaching or service differently further the reputation of the college or university?" Skeptics need little proof to stay put but a great deal of documentation that proposed changes end in the desired outcomes. People who resist change fear risk. They know the current system, and they are comfortable with it. Active resisters are the least likely to engage in change efforts. Deans who value harmony and collaboration need to recognize these faculty for what they do and move on. To enhance the college's integrity requires change. Deans who understand change stand a better chance of bringing it about (Katzenbach, 1998).[5] Appendix F lists several publications that may aid readers in understanding various concepts highlighted in the institutional integrity section.

What Can Universities Do to Help Deans Become More Effective?

R ECENTLY, THE AMERICAN COUNCIL on Education, Kellogg Commission (1999), Kellogg Foundation (1999), and the Global Consortium of Higher Education (Gmelch, 1999) each called for bolder and better college leadership. Deans alone, however, do not run effective colleges. Universities provide the broader context within which deans succeed or fail. As such, universities have a role to play in ensuring that their deans lead well. This final section provides ideas that can help universities further their deans' leadership abilities. Its components include selection, socialization, development, and evaluation. A final topic, rethinking the position, piques the imagination.

Universities have a role to play in ensuring that their deans lead well.

Selection of Deans

"One should select a colleague with only slightly less care than choosing a spouse. In fact, comparing tenure rates with divorce rates reveals that a choice of an academic colleague may well be more important" (Hynes, 1990, p. 52). This statement underscores the importance of decisions about hiring deans because deans directly impact the academic culture and college productivity.

Institutional searches for academic leaders often fail, with many of them going into second, third, or even fourth cycles. When positions remain unfilled, bad things happen: institutions suffer from a lack of leadership, colleges suffer from a lack of representation, faculty suffer from a lack of advocacy, states suffer from a lack of connection and communication, and the profession suffers from the void that is created (D. A. Andersen, 1999).

Blum (1994) suggests that the selection process itself is flawed. "The way I was chosen for the position . . . was reason enough not to . . . have taken [it] in the first place" (p. 160). Typically, after a search committee forms, an advertisement is placed in the *Chronicle of Higher Education* (Twombly, 1992). Committees then sit back and let the applications roll in. No one really knows whether the best qualified candidates end up in the pool. Marchese and Lawrence (1987) do provide a handbook that offers some assistance with the process, but few other resources exist.

Much of the search process follows the rituals, norms, and traditions of the institutions (Birnbaum, 1992). For instance, faculty and administrators usually make up search committees, and, in theory, each has a voice. In reality, faculty members may jockey for power and position with prospective deans, in some instances giving rise to questionable actions that verge on unethical behavior. Administrators on the committee make political choices, which are often taken more seriously than those of faculty. And if the university and the college have a viable internal candidate, the search becomes a costly, time-consuming sham for both the institution and the candidates (Blum, 1994; Lazerow and Winters, 1974; Newton, 1985; R. C. Phillips, 1969). To move beyond these shortcomings, the system—no matter what the process—must be strengthened.

The corporate world too bemoans the precarious state of executive selection. One executive commented, "I consider this selection decision one of the most devastating failures of my career" (Sessa and Taylor, 2000, p. 1). A host of reasons highlight why decision makers are unable or unwilling to select their organizations' next generation of leaders (Sessa and Taylor, 2000). First, they have little expertise in the selection of executives. Second, organizations may not employ the same rigor in selecting leaders that they do in other decision-making processes. Third, organizations have inadequate hiring, promotional, and succession-planning systems. And finally for higher education, the environment has changed dramatically and so have the demands for leadership. How can institutions of higher education respond to these deficiencies? Three strategies—reverse the process, look inside, and check the fit—provide universities with a place to start.

Reverse the Process

Universities are only as strong as their colleges, and colleges reflect the strength of their deans. And although provosts and presidents may not hold sole responsibility for recruiting deans, it must be one of their primary concerns. To this end, presidents and provosts could select deans, with faculty holding some power over the approval or disapproval of them. By doing so, the line of administrative responsibility becomes clearer, a great deal of faculty time is saved, and faculty are freer to point up a new dean's faults because they did not make the initial choice (Blum, 1994).

Look Inside

Conventional wisdom says that if organizations want change, they should bring someone new into the organization. This solution sometimes works. But Collins and Porras (1994) found that in more than 1,700 years of combined life spans across eighteen visionary companies, only four incidents (in two companies) involved outside hires. In effect, their study dispelled the myth that companies should hire outside CEOs to stimulate fundamental change. In comparison, less than one-half of dean positions are filled from within (Poskzim, 1984). External searches initiated in the fall and not disbanded until sometime in the spring take approximately seven months. Selection processes in the private sector differ significantly and appear to be more efficient, especially when candidates can be selected or promoted from within the organization. They take less time and involve fewer people in the decision. Universities might reconsider the necessity of external searches and, instead, grow their own deans.

Check the Fit

One-fifth of all deanships turn over each year. Part of this turnover stems from natural attrition in the position through advancement, relocation, or retirement. But a portion represents a lack of fit between institutions and their deans (Fenstermacher, 1995). Hiring deans to deal with fiscal crises but telling them they should be scholar-deans sets them up for failure because the qualifications of the latter do not necessarily meet the requirements of the former. Being clear about institutional expectations will go far in attracting and retaining the right person for the job (M. Wolverton, Gmelch, and Wolverton, 2000).

Even when the "perfect" candidate is selected, a dean's success is not guaranteed, because how deans transition into the position relates directly to college productivity. This transition actually involves two processes: (1) the socialization phase, which includes the anticipation before the assignment begins, transition into the position, and an adjustment period for both deans and colleges, and (2) the leadership development phase. We call attention to critical elements of each process as they relate to higher education.

Socialization of Deans

Organizational socialization spans three stages: anticipation, encounter, and adaptation (Hart, 1991). The anticipatory stage begins when a dean is selected for the new position and has made the decision to leave a current assignment. It is characterized by breaking off loyalties to the present institution and developing new ones. Louis (1980) refers to the process as "leave taking." The encounter stage unfolds when a dean actually starts the new position and begins to cope with its routines, surprises, and relationships. The adaptation stage begins when a dean develops strong trusting relationships in the college and finds out how things work in the informal organization. Research suggests that, in addition, deans may experience two other socializing stages—one at the beginning of the process when they first embrace the notion of seeking the deanship and reengagement at the end of the cycle as they settle into the deanship (Gmelch, 2000a; Gmelch and Parkay, 1999; Gmelch and Seedorf, 1989; Pollock, 1998). Studies of academic leaders and business executives point out that while many administrators successfully enter the anticipatory and encounter stages, few complete the adaptation stage and become fully socialized into administration (Gmelch and Parkay, 1999; Gmelch and Seedorf, 1989). Those who do successfully complete the process take anywhere from eighteen months (school principals, for example) to two and one-half years (business managers, for example) (Cosgrove, 1986; Gabarro, 1985; Lamoreaux, 1990; Weindling and Early, 1987). Those who fail to completely socialize into their positions remain in a mode of damage control, chaos, and conflict (Gmelch, 2000a, 2000b; Koch, 1968; Parkay and Hall, 1992; Pollock, 1998; Seedorf, 1990).

Deliberately or unconsciously, universities use a number of tactics to prepare deans for their new roles. We suggest that three relatively untapped options—encouraging mentorships, setting clear goals, and building networks for deans—deserve consideration.

Encouraging Mentorships

New deans experience socialization as individuals because they are usually the only new senior administrators entering the university at a given time and cannot be processed collectively as would be the case with new faculty (Straton-Spicer and Spicer, 1987). In addition, general orientation meetings provided for all new employees on benefits and university services fall short in terms of preparing deans for their new roles; they must learn the cultural and political ropes of the university through trial and error. Universities can help new deans acclimate to and learn about the context of their new positions by placing them under the mentorship of other deans and upper-level administrators within the system. This process can be quite formal with assigned individuals or even small committees, or informal yet university sponsored. In either instance, universities could provide some training for potential mentors to sensitize them to issues peculiar to particular disciplines or specific to women and minorities (Nies and Wolverton, 2000; Oakes, 1999).

Setting Clear Goals

In contrast to school principals, who receive a given sequence of discrete and identifiable steps leading to their position through administrative certification, deans experience random socialization as the steps and desired roles remain unknown, ambiguous, and, at times, continually changing. For deans, socialization has neither an identifiable beginning nor an end. They sometimes wander from year one into year two not knowing what, if anything, should have taken place. As a result, a great deal of ambiguity can arise for new deans. Universities can ease these problems and help deans learn the content of their positions by giving new initiates some preliminary but distinct indication of what should be accomplished within their first two or three years (M. Wolverton, Wolverton, and Gmelch, 1999).

Building Dean Networks

Socialization tactics provide a way of learning about networking within the institution. When deans follow in someone's footsteps and strong role models exist, they experience serial socialization. In some cases, deans enter as newcomers from the outside, and, while they may know their predecessors, many of these former deans remain distant so as not to interfere. Few provide what might be termed "extensive grooming" of the new dean. While stories and rituals of the previous dean are a rich part of the college culture, they do not have a significant influence on the new dean's socialization. Associate deans, assistants, and support staff who have served under previous deans do, however, guide new deans in learning the university and college nomenclature and protocol and a sense of university and college history and culture. Deans of other colleges within the university can serve as another reference point about the sociopolitical aspects of the university (Grossman, 1981; Prock, 1983). Such socialization helps, but over time deans have discovered that the best way to learn about how to improve performance is to get in a room with other deans for a day or two and discuss the problems they face and the solutions they have found (Gould, 1964). Universities can promote such networking opportunities for their deans by facilitating retreats and dialogues among deans within and across institutions.

At many universities today, deans confront a socialization process that is random and somewhat capricious, and they do so in isolation from other like-minded individuals. While this type of system can afford a great deal of flexibility for deans in determining their role, it can also seem akin to reading tea leaves. Those deans less adept at reading fail to understand the institution's informal cues (Gmelch, 2000b).

Leadership Development for Deans

Academic deans have been referred to as amateurs because they have not been prepared for their positions and many have no experience in the dean's office (A. E. Austin, 1984; M. F. Green, 1981; Jackson, 2000; Lamborn, 1991;

Marshall, 1956; R. A. Scott, 1979). To become an expert takes time. Studies in the corporate world show that truly productive managers take ten years to mature (Ericsson, Krampe, and Tesch-Romer, 1993). In the American university, seven years represents the threshold for faculty to attain the status of expert at the associate professor level and another seven years for full membership in the academy. If it takes up to fourteen years to achieve expertise in our academic disciplines, why do we assume we can create academic leaders with weekend seminars or half-day university orientation sessions? (Galbo, 1998).

For years, concerned parties have suggested that higher education needs a radical change in its approach to leadership development (Jackson, 2000; Kellogg Foundation, 1999; Lamborn, 1991; Schuh, 1974). Businesses have found that leadership preparation requires a combination of socialization, which inculcates leaders with the values and vision of the institution; individual skill development, which equips them with the tools of leadership; and strategic interventions, which provide experience (Conger and Benjamin, 1999).

Skill Development

In longitudinal studies, new managers noted that they did not have the self-confidence to aspire to general management jobs until they had acquired three kinds of competence: analytical competence, to recognize and formulate problems to be worked on; interpersonal competence, to build and maintain various kinds of relationships and groups; and emotional competence, to handle the emotional demands of the managerial role itself (Schein, 1985, p. 171). This search for competence may also be a primary challenge for new deans.

Seminars and professional development materials are available to deans but scarce. Most of the leadership development efforts for deans are sponsored by professional associations such as the American Council on Education, the American Association of Colleges for Teacher Education, the Council of Colleges of Arts and Sciences, the American Association of Colleges and Schools of Business, and the American Association of Colleges of Nursing. Additional insight can be gained from books such as *Deaning: Middle Management in Academe* (Morris, 1981), *The Academic Dean: Dove, Dragon, and Diplomat* (Tucker and Bryan, 1988), *Investing in Higher Education: A Handbook of Leadership Development* (M. F. Green and McDade, 1994), *The University: An Owner's Manual* (Rosovsky, 1990), and *Resource Handbook for*

Academic Deans (Allan, 1999). But while these resources represent perspectives on the deanship, they do not provide deans with the skills they require.

Deans and researchers suggest three specific areas of skill development—communication, conflict resolution, and team building—as crucial to the deanship (Darling and Pomatto, 1999; Grossman, 1981; Kritek, 1994). In the first instance, deans have years of writing experience. The type of writing in which they engage as administrators, however, must be more direct, concise, and readable. The object becomes getting ideas down on paper in enough words to express them fully but not so many that no one reads it. Similarly, many deans have well developed oratory skills. But in administration, the focus moves from classroom lectures and research and meeting presentations to policy-based speeches before legislators and funding agencies. In addition, the art of persuasion becomes well honed as deans make the case for their colleges to central administration (S. L. Barker, 1984; Conger, 1998). Likewise, some are good listeners. As deans move into the political arena, listening entails searching for nuances that tell of emotional distress, tension, or hidden agendas, falsehoods that build off half-truths and could damage the college, and outright lies and deception (Lawler, 1992; McCaskey, 1979; S. C. Smith and Piele, 1997; Steil, Baker, and Watson, 1983). The combination of all three of these redefined communication skills (writing, persuasion, and listening) makes deans effective (Grossman, 1981).

In the second, deans deal with conflict daily. Whether they can do so effectively in part determines the health of their colleges. A former dean suggests that deans constantly encounter power differentials when they negotiate or mediate differences, especially among diverse constituencies (Kritek, 1994). In *Negotiating at an Uneven Table,* she delineates ten ways of being at the table—with authenticity, truthfulness, integrity, persistence, compassion, innovativeness, self-awareness, an understanding of the context, the ability to take a stance, and the knowledge of when and how to leave the table.

In the third, team building requires more than putting a group of people in a room and closing the door. Deans need to understand behavioral styles, have an awareness of how people with different styles interact, and be able to capture the strengths of team members in ways that compensate for personal and team members' weaknesses (Darling and Pomatto, 1999; Hecht, Higgerson,

Gmelch, and Tucker, 1999). The responsibilities of the deanship in many colleges can no longer be shouldered by one individual. They are too complex and require disparate types of knowledge and skill that no one person can hope to possess. Building a strong leadership team of associate and assistant deans, directors, business managers, and department chairs (or some combination thereof) becomes an imperative (Heenan and Bennis, 1999). One useful team schematic differentiates team members as contributors who provide teams with technical information and data; collaborators who are flexible and work to keep teams focused

> **The responsibilities of the deanship in many colleges can no longer be shouldered by one individual.**

on goals; communicators who facilitate the process by listening, providing feedback, and building consensus; and challengers who play the devil's advocate, questioning goals, methods, and ethics and encouraging calculated risk taking. The ideal team has representatives from all four groups (Parker, 1996).

Universities can ensure that deans possess these skills by encouraging them to sit in on courses offered in their business and education colleges. They can also send them to institutes, such as Harvard's management development program and Bryn Mawr's program for new and aspiring female administrators. Finally, universities can assemble and provide survival reference libraries to all deans.

Experience

Transitioning into leadership is not an easy process. It requires understanding organizational nuances and being able to build and sustain relationships. In short, it takes experience. Gabarro (1985) discovered that the single most salient factor in differentiating successful from failed transitions was the quality of a leader's working relationships by the end of the first year. If leaders had trouble establishing sound partnerships in the workplace, trust was eventually breached and they could not get beyond initial socialization phases. This situation is not unique to businesses. A university center director recently commented, "It is much easier to transfer knowledge and power than it is to transfer relationships. . . . This continues to be the hardest part of the transition for me" (Sorenson, 2000, p. 140).

Over the years, deans and researchers have suggested several ways in which universities might speed up the acquisition of knowledge deans gain through experience. For instance, universities can arrange for internships where new deans serve as apprentices or shadows to more experienced ones (A. E. Austin, 1984; M. Wolverton and Gonzales, 2000). Gould (1964) suggested that upon hiring new deans, universities should give them a semester-long sabbatical and send them to at least three different institutions to observe other deans. Similarly, Poch and Wolverton (2000) proposed corporate executive-dean exchanges where business leaders gain an appreciation for the uniqueness and value of higher education institutions and deans are exposed to effective business practices. Universities might also attempt to overlap terms of retiring deans who have proven track records with those of their replacements by one semester, giving new deans the opportunity to gain a better understanding of college operation (Gould, 1964). Finally, universities might think of higher education as a national institution and work cooperatively across institutions to create a cadre of potential deans well prepared for leadership (Gmelch, Wolverton, Wolverton, and Sarros, 1999; Yingling, 1981). In each instance, deans establish foundations upon which credible work relationships can be built.

Selection of deans and dean transition (socialization and development) are interconnected. Simply put, one cannot be accomplished well in isolation from the other. While universities must determine what candidates can bring to an organization, they must also determine what the organization can do to support and develop potential deans (Sessa and Taylor, 2000).

Evaluation

Little can be said about the evaluation of deans (Seldin, 1988). A former nursing dean at a Research I university captured it best. "After five years, I asked the chancellor about my evaluation and was told, 'You don't know it but we're evaluating you everyday.' After 10 years, I asked again. The response was: 'How old are you?' '60.' 'I think you'll make it . . . '" (Prock, 1983, p. 15). Part of creating strong and healthy leadership in any organization entails letting people know how they are doing, if for no other reason than it reinforces good habits and points up bad ones. Deans need the freedom to make mistakes. Without clear guidelines that demonstrate the criteria by which they will be judged, they may avoid risks they should be taking.

Universities can begin by building assessment approaches around three general categories—performance, relationships, and results. Performance indicators are the easiest to define and measure. Alone, they cannot, however, differentiate successful from unsuccessful deans. Nor does the ability to build and maintain relationships or get results tell us who is effective. Universities make mistakes when they focus on one component in isolation from the other two.

Without clear guidelines that demonstrate the criteria by which they will be judged, [deans] may avoid risks they should be taking.

Indicators for each of these categories can be tailored to reflect concerns unique to a dean's academic discipline, but generally they revolve around common college dimensions, such as budget, students, faculty productivity, service, accreditation, and the college's contribution to the greater good of the university (Grossman, 1981; Sessa and Taylor, 2000). For instance, indicators of performance include, but are not limited to, pursuing ideas, making accurate forecasts, following through on commitments, selecting staff, managing resources, making policy, being organized, and speaking well in public.

Such indicators provide provosts with snapshots of a dean's performance, but a dean's relationships, especially with faculty and staff, determine productivity (results) (Pfeffer and Viega, 1999). Simply put, a dean's ability to nurture, stretch, grow, evaluate, and tell people when the fit is wrong ultimately determines college and university health (Lasley and Haberman, 1987; Sessa and Taylor, 2000). Such relational skills develop over time, and in reality brief pictures of performance cannot accurately capture the essence of effective leadership. Overall work environment, assessed by faculty and staff, and movement toward institutional goals, determined by upper administration, represent measurable indicators that connect relationships and results and complement performance measures.

Heck, Johnsrud, and Rosser (1999) experimented with a mechanism for monitoring deans' performance that roughly approximates a three-category system. Within a multicampus university system, they calculated faculty and staff ratings of deans' effectiveness along seven dimensions: communication skills, college management, and college leadership (performance); interpersonal relationships and support of institutional diversity (relationships); and quality of education provided by the college and research/professional endeavors (results). Early findings suggest that such a system (we suggest coupled with a provost's view of performance and results) has merit.[6]

Rethinking the Position

Professional development seminars and training in time management may help "fix" the dean. The truly committed dean might even enroll in an executive MBA program, which may provide a viable remedy to the leadership (or at least the management) question. Deans can also learn to maintain balance between their professional and personal lives. We cannot assume, however, that fixing the dean will completely alleviate the problem. The larger issue may rest with colleges and universities. And for deans to remain effective as leaders and administrators, institutions must respond. Clear signals must be sent about institutional priorities, because to continually expand the responsibilities of the position only weakens it. Colleges and universities must think in terms of redefining the position and the organization of work. Ultimately, careful examination of the position could lead to its restructuring.

Institutions steeped in tradition rarely take time to rethink positions of authority and organizational structure. Such a move, however, might prove fruitful for universities. Deans today oversee professional organizations (colleges) that are in some ways similar to large professional partnerships or organizations in the private sector, such as those found in law and accounting firms. And these partnerships operate within the greater enterprise (or partnership) we call the university. Often the responsibilities exceed one person's management and leadership capacity.

Team leadership, in its purest sense although rare, is by no means a new concept in business. In 1991, Nordstrom, Inc. created a co-presidency comprising four nonfamily members. This effort at shared leadership was instigated in an effort to pull the national retailer out of a slump. These co-presidents described their functions as concentrating "on different parts of the business, but on company matters speak[ing] with one voice" (Schwadel, 1991). Although Nordstrom's co-CEOship has undergone several executive shifts—adding family CEOs to share the position, removing all family members down to two, returning to one CEO, and most recently in September 2000, removing the sole CEO and reinstating a four-family-member co-CEO (Spurgeon, 2000)—Nordstrom, Inc. shows no hesitation at the thought of sharing the leadership responsibilities for the good of the company (Wolverton, Montez, and Gmelch, 2000).

Likewise, Charles Schwab Corp., an investment brokerage firm, now employs co-CEOs to jointly handle the responsibilities of president (David Pottruck) and chair (Charles Schwab) (McGeehan, 1997). The investment banking business of Goldman, Sachs and Co. also has a history of using co-leaders to run the corporation amid a collegial culture. Those who have succeeded at Goldman, Sachs, Stephen Friedman and Robert Rubin, for instance, stress the importance of "compatible chemistry" and conducting the sharing aspect of the title as "giving of one's self and ideas to the other while being responsive of [the other's] needs" (Lublin and Schellhardt, 1998, p. C14).

In 1997, Centigram Corporation, a communication technology company, created an interim co-CEOship while it sought a permanent CEO. The two-person team comprised the general manager/executive vice president (whose strengths were in sales and marketing) and the CFO (whose strength lay in operations). These two individuals jointly exercised their respective expertise in day-to-day executive functions. Benefits of this arrangement were that responsibilities were divided and assumed according to strengths, making for efficient operations and a decreased sense of being overwhelmed in the job. Disadvantages were that the necessity for constant communication often slowed the decision-making process and departments often made end runs around the "two-headed dragon" of leadership. The conjoint nature of this arrangement, however, is summed up by one of the co-CEOs: "It [is] very important that the co-CEOs not become disjointed and not let people get in between them. . . . In order for any 'co-' relationship to work, both people have to have egos that don't need to be number 1. If ego becomes a factor, one will try to destroy the other person, or at least make them look bad in some way" (Wolverton, Montez, and Gmelch, 2000, p. 19).

Even educators are beginning to test the waters. Several years ago, A. E. Austin (1984) suggested that universities look at innovative arrangements of workloads. In 1999, the graduate school of education at Harvard revealed its approach to the innovation of a co-deanship: two administrators share the position, an office with two desks and two computers, and a joint space for meetings. They share the work and the salary stipend and continue to work jointly on research ("Peer Review," 1999, p. A14). It takes a special type of person to engage in a co-deanship, but who is to say whether or not in the right situation the arrangement might provide a viable alternative to conventional deanships.

One Final Thought

Mary Catherine Bateson, a former liberal arts and sciences dean, once reflected, "Being a new dean is like learning to ice skate in full view of your faculty." Universities assume, or perhaps hope, that deans can lead colleges but do little to help prepare them for that role and give them sparse and sometimes ambiguous feedback during their careers as deans. If the primary responsibility of deans is to create college cultures conducive to collegiality and productivity, then they must learn to recognize and cope with the stages of their own leadership development and the challenges they face. Ultimately, universities and deans must work together to provide effective leadership for the future. We believe that we have provided a starting point. The rest is up to universities and their deans. As an old Buddhist philosopher once said, "To know and not to use, is not yet to know."

Ultimately, universities and deans must work together to provide effective leadership for the future.

Appendix A: Diversity Resources for Deans

Adams, M., Bell, L. A., & Griffin, P. (Eds.). (1997). *Teaching for diversity and social justice: A sourcebook.* New York: Routledge.

This book provides an understanding of what it takes to integrate an appreciation of diversity into a college curriculum beginning with engaging college members in conversation around the issue. For example, Tatum suggests an exercise, called Common Ground, that she often uses to begin such dialogues. In *Common Ground,* participants line up on one side of the room. Tatum, then, reads a series of 15 to 20 statements that identify groups. These might include: I am a woman; I am Latino; I am Jewish; I am an immigrant; I grew up poor; I have a disability; and so on. As participants hear an identifier that pertains to them, they silently cross to the other side of the room, look to see who crossed with them and who remained behind, and then return to their original places. The exercise provides powerful reminders of whose voices are not represented in the room, who stands alone and isolated, and what people have in common. An exercise like this in a retreat setting can bring issues for discussion to the surface, allow a group to feel a sense of intimacy, and provide valuable background information to those involved.

Aguirre, Jr., A. (2000). *Women and minority faculty in the academic workplace: Recruitment, retention, and academic culture.* ASHE-ERIC Higher Education Report 27(6). San Francisco: Jossey-Bass.

Cox, Jr., T. (1994). *Cultural diversity in organizations: Theory, research and practice.* San Francisco: Berrett-Koehler. See also Cox, T. & Beale, R. (1997). *Developing competency to manage diversity: Readings, cases and activities.* San Francisco: Berrett-Koehler.

Gardenswartz, L., & Rowe, A. (1993). *Managing diversity: A complete desk reference and planning guide.* New York: IRWIN/Pfeiffer & Company.

Hurtado, S., Milem, J., Clayton-Pedersen, A., & Allen, W. (1999). *Enacting diverse learning environments: Improving the climate for racial/ethnic diversity in higher education.* (Vol. 26, no. 8). Washington, DC: The George Washington University, Graduate School of Education and Human Development.

Authors suggest strategies that deans might use in moving their colleges toward a more global understanding, acceptance, and celebration of diversity. One example that they feature is Vanderbilt's Diversity Opportunity Tools. This research-based program can be used individually or by groups. It is computerized and interactive and designed to help people learn how to deal with inappropriate behavior that derives from ignorance or manifests itself because expected behaviors remain unclear (Hurtado and others, 1999).

Appendix B: Law Resources for Deans

Books

Alexander, K., & Solomon, E. S. (1972). *College and university law.* Charlottesville, VA: Michie Co.

Kaplin, W. A. & Lee, B. A. (1995). *The law of higher education.* San Francisco: Jossey-Bass.

Olivas, M. A. (1997). *The law and higher education.* Durham, NC: Carolina Academic Press.

Russo, C. J. (ed.) (1999). *Yearbook of education law, 1999.* Dayton, OH: Education Law Association.

Stevens, E. (1999). *Due process and higher education: A systemic approach to fair decision making.* ASHE-ERIC Higher Education Report 27(2). Washington, DC: The George Washington University, Graduate School of Education and Human Development.

Toma, J. D. & Palm, R. L. (1999). *The academic administrator and the law: What every dean and department chair needs to know.* ASHE-ERIC Higher Education Report 26(5). Washington, DC: The George Washington University, Graduate School of Education and Human Development.

Weeks, K. M. (1982). *Legal deskbook for administrators of independent colleges and universities.* Notre Dame, IN: Center for Constitutional Studies, Notre Dame Law School.

Journals

The Journal of College and University Law publishes articles on current issues in higher education law.

Associations

National Association of College and University Attorneys (NACUA)
   Website: www.nacua.org
College and University Personnel Association (CUPA)
   Website: www.cupahr.org

National Association of Student Personnel Administrators (NASPA)
 Website: www.naspa.org
American College Personnel Association (ACPA)
 Website: www.acpa.nche.edu

Appendix C: Technology Resources for Deans

Publications

Bates, A. W. (2000). *Managing technological change: Strategies for college and university leaders.* San Francisco: Jossey-Bass.

Noam, E. (1995). Electronics and the dim future of the university. *Science, 270,* 247–249.

Perelman, L. (1993). *School's out: Hyperlearning, the new technology, and the end of education.* New York: Knopf.

Van Dusen, G. C. (1997). *The virtual campus: Technology and reform in higher education.* ASHE-ERIC Higher Education Report 25(5). Washington, DC: The George Washington University.

Van Dusen, G. C. (2000). *Digital dilemma: Issues of access, cost, and quality in media- enhanced and distance education.* ASHE-ERIC Higher Education Report 27(5). San Francisco: Jossey-Bass.

Programs

The Flashlight Program helps educators and organizations carry out technology planning and implementation projects. Contact the program at their Web site or by email.

www.tltgroup.org/programs/flashlight.html

    email: flashlight@tltgroup.org

Appendix D: Finance and Budgeting Resources for Deans

For those deans interested in understanding the economics of higher education and its implications for funding and budgeting, somewhat dated but still relevant resources include:

Cohen E. & Geske, T. G. (1990). *The economics of education.* New York: Pergamon Press.

Hoenach, S. A. & Colllins, E. L. (eds.) (1990). *The economics of American universities.* New York: SUNY.

More current resources include:

Breneman, D. W., Leslie, L. L. & Anderson, R. E. (eds.) (1996). *ASHE reader on finance in higher education.* Needham Heights, MA: Simon and Schuster.

Callan, P. M., Finney, J. E., Bracco, K. R., and Doyle, W. R. (1997). *Public and private financing of higher education: Shaping public policy for the future.* Phoenix: American Council on Education and Oryx Press.

Finkelstein, M. J., Frances, C., Jewett, F. I. & Scholz, B. W. (2000). *Dollars, distance, and online education: The new economies of college teaching and learning.* Phoenix: American Council on Education and Oryx Press.

Meisinger, R. J., Jr. (1994). *College and university budgeting: An introduction for faculty and academic administrators.* Washington DC: National Association of College and University Business Officers.

Sturtevant, W. T. (1997). *The artful journey: Cultivating and soliciting the major gift.* Chicago: Bonus Books.

Appendix E: Survival Tools for Deans Seeking Balance

Blanchard, K. & Johnson, S. (1986). *One minute manager.* New York: Berkley Books.

Cottrell, D. & Layton, M. C. (2000). *175 ways to get more done in less time.* Dallas: Cornerstone Leadership Institute.

Rockhurst College Continuing Education Center, Inc. (1995). *Self-profile: A guide for positive interpersonal communication.* Shawnee Mission, KS: National Press Publications.

Rockhurst College Continuing Education Center, Inc. (1997). *Powerful communication skills: how to communicate with confidence, clarity and credibility.* Shawnee Mission, KS: National Press Publications.

Rockhurst College Continuing Education Center, Inc. (1995). *The stress management handbook: A practical guide to reducing stress in every aspect of your life.* Shawnee Mission, KS: National Press Publications.

Appendix F: Ideas for Deans on Organizational Integrity

Revisiting Change Leadership

Johari Window

	I Know	I Don't Know
They Know	I say I support teaching.	My actions don't support my words.
They Don't Know	I really mean it.	What's behind the gap above?

For the dean who wants to improve teaching, both may know that the dean says he/she supports teaching (Quadrant 1), but while the dean knows he/she really means it, the faculty may not (Quadrant 2). The dean, in this instance, probably does not realize that his/her actions do not support what is being said (Quadrant 3). Neither the dean nor faculty quite know why the gap in Quadrant 3 exists (Quadrant 4).

For more in depth information on redefining faculty work, reframing academic departments, and academic scorecards, see:

Krahenbuhl, G. (1998). Faculty work: Integrating responsibilities and institutional needs. *Change, 30*(6), 18–25.

O'Neil, H. J., Jr., Bensimon, E. M., Diamond, M. A. & Moore, M. R. (1999). Designing and implementing an academic scorecard. *Change, 31*(6), 32–41.

Walvoord, B. E., and others. (2000). Academic departments: How they work, how they change. *ASHE-ERIC Higher Education Report 27*(8). San Francisco: Jossey-Bass.

Wolverton, M. Gmelch, W. H. & Sorenson, D. (1998). The department as double agent: The call for departmental change and renewal. *Innovative Higher Education, 22*(3), 203–215.

For a quick reference on change in the workplace, see:

Costello, S. J. (1994). *Managing change in the workplace.* Burr Ridge, IL: Irvin Professional Publishing, Mirror Press.

Appendix G: A Survival Reference Library for Deans

Business-Oriented Writing Resources

Elbow, P. (1981). *Writing with power.* New York: Oxford University Press.

O'Connor, P. (2000). When *words fail me: What everyone who writes should know about writing.* New York: Harvest Books.

Strunk Jr., W. & White, E. B. (1979). *Elements of style* (3d ed.). Needham Heights, MA: Allyn & Bacon.

Public Speaking

Parkhurst, W. (1988). *The eloquent executive.* New York: Times Books.

Minnick, W. C. (1968). *The art of persuasion.* Boston: Houghton Mifflin.

Conflict Resolution and Negotiation

Kritek, P. B. (1994). *Negotiating at an uneven table: A practical approach to working with difference and diversity.* San Francisco: Jossey-Bass.

Fisher, R. & Ury, W. (1981). *Getting to yes: Negotiating agreement without giving in.* New York: Penguin Books.

Ury, W. (1993). *Getting past no: Negotiating your way from confrontation to cooperation.* New York: Bantam Books.

Teamwork

Katzenbach, J. R. & Smith, D. K. (1993). *The wisdom of teams: Creating the high-performance organization.* Boston: Harvard Business School Press.

Parker, G. (1996). *Team players and teamwork: The new competitive business strategy.* San Francisco: Jossey-Bass.

General Overview of the Deanship

Wolverton, M., Gmelch, W. H., Montez, J. & Nies, C. T. (2001). *The changing nature of the academic deanship.* ASHE ERIC Report Series. San Francisco: Jossey-Bass.

Notes

[1]As recently as 1996, for instance, deans remained predominantly male. In only four of thirty-one disciplines (health-related professions, home economics, nursing, and special programs) did females dominate. Female deans were overwhelmingly in the minority in the "status" professions such as business, law, medicine, engineering, pharmacy, veterinary medicine, and dentistry (Glazer-Raymo, 1999).

[2]Gould (1964) conducted research on 180 liberal arts deans, interviewing 14 deans and surveying another 166; Griffiths and McCarty (1980) looked at 181 education deans. Moore (1982) used data from the Leaders in Transition Project to examine a randomly selected sample of 2,896 administrators, of which 653 deans constituted a subset. Moore's study focused on gender and minority representation and career trajectory. Miller (1989) surveyed 244 business deans.

[3]In this particular project, roughly 800 deans from four academic disciplines (education, liberal arts and sciences, nursing, and business) at three types of universities (research, comprehensive, and baccalaureate), both public and private, responded to an in-depth questionnaire.

[4]In particular, see Baez and Centra (1995), Dilts, Haber, and Bialik (1994), and Tierney (1998).

[5]For more in-depth information on redefining faculty work, reframing academic departments, and using academic scorecards, see Krahenbuhl (1998), O'Neil, Bensimon, Diamond, & Moore (1999), and M. Wolverton, Gmelch, & Sorenson (1998). For a quick reference on change in the workplace, see Costello (1994).

[6]See Edwards (1999), Erhlich (2000), Hecht, Higgerson, Gmelch, and Tucker (1999), Krahenbuhl (1998), North (1995), O'Neil, Bensimon, Diamond, and Moore (1999), and Ramaley (2000) for ideas about department, chair, and college evaluation that could be adapted to deans.

[6]See Edwards (1999), Erhlich (2000), Hecht, Higgerson, Gmelch, and Tucker (1999), Krahenbuhl (1998), North (1995), O'Neil, Bensimon, Diamond, and Moore (1999), and Ramaley (2000) for ideas about department, chair, and college evaluation that could be adapted to deans.

References

Abramson, L. W., and Moss, G. M. (1977). Law school deans: A self portrait. *Journal of Legal Education, 29,* 6–30.

Adams, M., Bell, L. A., and Griffin, P. (Eds.). (1997). *Teaching for diversity and social justice: A sourcebook.* New York: Routledge.

Aguirre, A., Jr. (2000). *Women and minority faculty in the academic workplace: Recruitment, retention, and academic culture* (ASHE-ERIC Higher Education Report 27(6)). San Francisco: Jossey-Bass.

Albert, L. S. (1994). Beyond ourselves: An interview with AAHE board chair Helen Astin. *AAHE Bulletin, 47*(1), 10–12.

Alexander, K., and Solomon, E. S. (1972). *College and university law.* Charlottesville, VA: Michie Co.

Allan, G. (Ed.). (1999). *The resource handbook for academic deans.* Washington, DC: American Conference of Academic Deans.

Allen, C. (1996). Corporations grow their own best employees at corporate universities. *Journal of Career Planning & Employment, 56,* 24–27.

Allen-Meares, P. (1997). Serving as dean: A public university perspective. New Directions for Higher Education, vol. 25(2). San Francisco: Jossey-Bass.

Alstete, J. W. (2000). *Posttenure faculty development* (ASHE-ERIC Higher Education Report 27(4)). San Francisco: Jossey-Bass.

Amabile, T. M. (1998, September-October). How to kill creativity. *Harvard Business Review,* 77–87.

Andersen, D. A. (1999). *Deans of the future.* Paper presented at the Conference of the American Association of Colleges of Teacher Education, Washington, DC.

Andersen, D. G., and King, J. P. (1987). The dean of education: A demographic analysis. *Journal of Teacher Education, 38*(5), 9–12.

Arends, R. (1998). Building capacity for change. In D. Thiessen and K. R. Howey (Eds.), *Agents, provocateurs: Reform-minded leaders for schools of education.* Washington, DC: American Association of Colleges for Teacher Education.

Association of Governing Boards of Universities and Colleges. (1996). *Ten public policy issues for higher education in 1996.* Washington, DC: Association of Governing Boards of Universities and Colleges.

Astin, A. W. (1993). *What matters in college? Four critical years revisited.* San Francisco: Jossey-Bass.

Astin, H. (1996, July-August). Leadership for social change. *About Campus,* 4–10.

Astin, H. S., and Astin, A. W. (1996). *A social change model of leadership development guidebook. Version III.* Los Angeles: UCLA Higher Education Research Institute.

Athena University. (1999). *Home page.* Available: http://www.athena.edu.

Austin, A. E. (1984). The work experience of university and college administrators. *American Association of University Administrators, 6*(1), 1–6.

Austin, M. J., Ahearn, F. L., and English, R. A. (1997a). Guiding organizational change. In M. J. Austin, F. L. Ahearn, and R. A. English (Eds.), *The professional dean: Meeting the leadership challenges* (pp. 31–56). San Francisco: Jossey-Bass.

Austin, M. J., Ahearn, F. L., and English, R. A. (Eds.). (1997b). *The professional dean: Meeting the leadership challenges.* San Francisco: Jossey-Bass.

Avolio, B., and Bass, B. (1988). Transformational leadership, charisma, and beyond. In J. G. Hunt, B. R. Baliga, H. P. Dachler, and C. A. Schriesheim (Eds.), *Emerging leadership vistas.* Lexington, MA: Lexington Books.

Baez, B., and Centra, J. A. (1995). *Tenure, promotion, and reappointment: Legal and administrative implications.* (ASHE-ERIC Higher Education Report, no. 1). Washington, DC: School of Education and Human Development, George Washington University.

Baker, W. J., and Gloster, A., II. (1994). Moving toward the virtual university: A vision of technology in higher education. *Cause/Effect, 17,* 4–11.

Banks, J. A. (Ed.). (1995). *Handbook of research on multicultural education.* New York: Macmillan.

Bardaracco, J. L., Jr. (1998, March-April). The discipline of building character. *Harvard Business Review,* 115–124.

Barker, D. I. (1994). A technological revolution in higher education. *Journal of Educational Technology Systems, 23*(2), 155–168.

Barker, S. L. (1984). *The influence of academic deans on colleagues and superiors.* Paper presented at the Conference on Postsecondary Education sponsored by the Association for the Study of Higher Education and the American Educational Research Association Division J, San Francisco, CA.

Barnard, J. (1997). The World Wide Web and higher education: The promise of virtual universities and online libraries. *Educational Technology, 37*(3), 30–35.

Barzun, J. M. (1945, February). Deans within deans. *Atlantic Monthly, 175,* 76.

Bass, B. M. (1985). *Leadership and performance beyond expectations.* New York: Free Press.

Bass, B. M. (1998). *Transformational leadership: Industrial, military and educational impact.* Mahwah, NJ: Erlbaum.

Bates, A.W.T. (2000). *Managing technological change: Strategies for college and university leaders.* San Francisco: Jossey-Bass.

Batson, T., and Bass, R. (1996). Primacy of process: Teaching and learning in the computer age. *Change, 28*(2), 42–47.

Bauer, R. C. (1955). *Cases in college administration.* New York: Bureau of Publications, Teachers College, Columbia University.

Belenky, M. F., Clinchy, B. M., Goldberger, N. R., and Tarule, J. M. (1986). *Women's ways of knowing: The development of self, voice, and mind.* New York: Basic Books.

Bennis, W. (1999). *Managing people is like herding cats.* Provo, UT: Executive Excellence Publishing.

Bennis, W. G., and Nanus, B. (1985). *Leaders: The strategies for taking charge.* New York: Harper & Row.

Bensimon, E. M., and Neumann, A. (1993). *Redesigning collegiate leadership: Teams and teamwork in higher education.* Baltimore: Johns Hopkins University Press.

Bensimon, E. M., Neumann, A., and Birnbaum, R. (1989). *Making sense of administrative leadership: The "L" word in higher education* (AAHE-ERIC Higher Education Report, no. 1). Washington, DC: George Washington University.

Bergquist, W. H. (1992). *The four cultures of the academy: Insights and strategies for improving leadership in collegiate organizations.* San Francisco: Jossey-Bass.

Birnbaum, R. (1990). *How colleges work: The cybernetics of academic organization and leadership.* San Francisco: Jossey-Bass.

Birnbaum, R. (1992). *How academic leadership works: Understanding success and failure in the college presidency.* San Francisco: Jossey-Bass.

Blanchard, K., and Johnson, S. (1986). *One-minute manager.* New York: Berkley Books.

Blum, A. A. (1994). Faculty searches for administrators: A reevaluation. *Contemporary Education, 65*(3), 160–162.

Boettcher, J. V. (2000). How much does it cost to put a course online? It all depends. In M. J. Finkelstein, C. Frances, F. I. Jewett, and B. W. Scholz (Eds.), *Dollars, distance, and online education: The new economics of college teaching and learning* (pp. 172–198). Phoenix, AZ: ACE/Oryx Press.

Bogue, E. G. (1994). *Leadership by design: Strengthening integrity in higher education.* San Francisco: Jossey-Bass.

Bok, D. (1992). Reclaiming the public trust. *Change, 24*(4), 12–19.

Bowen, H. R. (1977). *Investment in learning: The individual and social value of American higher education.* San Francisco: Jossey-Bass.

Bower, F. (1993). Women and maundering in higher education. In Mitchell, P. T. (Ed.), *Cracking the wall: Women in higher education administration* (pp. 91–97). Washington, DC: College and University Personnel Association.

Bowker, L. H. (1982a). The academic dean: A descriptive study. *Teaching Sociology, 9*(3), 257–271.

Bowker, L. H. (1982b). The college dean: A case of miscommunication about the importance of teaching. *Liberal Education, 67,* 319–326.

Boyer Commission on Educating Undergraduates in Research Universities. (1998). *Reinventing undergraduate education: A blueprint for America's research universities.* Stony Brook, NY: State University of New York.

Boyer, E. (1990a). *Campus life: In search of community.* Princeton, NJ: Carnegie Foundation for the Advancement of Teaching.

Boyer, E. (1990b). *Scholarship reconsidered: Priorities of the professoriate.* Princeton, NJ: Carnegie Foundation for the Advancement of Teaching.

Boyer, E. (1996). The scholarship of enjoyment. *Journal of Public Service and Outreach, 1*(1).

Boyer, E., and Mitgang, L. (1996). *Building community: A new future for architectural education and practice*. Princeton, NJ: Carnegie Foundation.

Bradford, D. L., and Cohen, A. R. (1998). *Power up: Transforming organizations through shared leadership*. New York: Wiley.

Breneman, D. W., Leslie, L. L., and Anderson, R. E. (Eds.). (1996). *ASHE reader on finance in higher education*. Needham Heights, MA: Simon & Schuster.

Brewer, K. C. (1995). *The stress management handbook: A practical guide to reducing stress in every aspect of your life*. Shawnee Mission, KS: National Press Publications.

Brittingham, B. E., and Pezzullo, T. R. (1990). *The campus green: Fund raising in higher education*. Washington, DC: School of Education and Human Resources, George Washington University.

Bronstein, P., Rothblum, E., and Solomon, S. (1993). Ivy halls and glass walls: Barriers to academic careers for women and ethnic minorities. In J. Gainen and R. Boice (Eds.), *Building a diverse faculty*. San Francisco: Jossey-Bass.

Brown, J. S. (2000). Growing up digital: How the web changes work, education, and the ways people learn. *Change, 32*(2), 10–21.

Brown, J. S., and Duguid, P. (1996). Universities in the digital age. *Change, 28*(4), 10–19.

Brubacher, J. S., and Rudy, W. (1958). *Higher education in transition*. New York: Harper & Row.

Burgos-Sasscer, R. (1990). *The changing face of leadership: The role of Hispanics*. Paper presented at the Annual International Conference on Leadership Development of the League for Innovation in the Community College, San Francisco, CA.

Burns, J. M. (1978). *Leadership*. New York: Harper & Row.

Caelleigh, A. S. (1993). Credit and responsibility in scientific authorship. In D. L. Cheney (Ed.), *Ethical issues in research* (pp. 45–55). Frederick, MD: University Publishing Group.

Cahn, S. M. (1997). The missing step in searches for academic administrators. *AAHE Bulletin, 50*(2), 7–9.

California Higher Education Policy Center. (1994). *Three strikes could undermine college opportunity*. San Jose, CA: ERIC. (ED 406 937)

Callan, P. M., Finney, J. E., Bracco, K. R., and Doyle, W. R. (Eds.). (1997). *Public and private financing of higher education: Shaping public policy for the future*. Phoenix, AZ: ACE/Oryx Press.

Camic, C. (1992). The matter of habit. In M. Zey (Ed.), *Decision making: Alternatives to rational choice models*. Thousand Oaks, CA: Sage Publications.

Cantor, J. A. (2000). *Higher education outside of the academy* (ASHE-ERIC Higher Education Report 27(7)). San Francisco: Jossey-Bass.

Cantú-Weber, J. (1999). Harassment and discrimination: News stories show litigation on the rise. *Change, 31*(3), 38–45.

Caplan, R. D. (1983). Person-environment fit: Past, present, and future. In C. L. Cooper (Ed.), *Stress research* (pp. 35–78). New York: Wiley.

Caplan, R. D., and others. (1980). *Job demands and worker health: Main effects and occupational differences*. Ann Arbor: University of Michigan.

Caplow, T., and McGee, R. J. (1958). *The academic marketplace*. New York: Basic Books.

Carbone, R. F. (1987). *Fund raisers of academe* (Monograph no. 1). College Park: Clearinghouse for Research on Fund Raising, University of Maryland.

Carnegie Foundation for the Advancement of Teaching. (1990). *Campus life: In search of community.* Princeton, NJ: Carnegie Foundation.

Carr, D., Hard, K., and Trahant, W. (1996). *Managing the change process: A field guide for change agents, consultants, team leaders and reengineering managers.* New York: McGraw-Hill.

Cashman, K. (1999). *Leadership from the inside out: Becoming a leader for life.* Provo, UT: Executive Excellence Publishing.

Castenell, L. A., and Tarule, J. A. (Eds.). (1997). *The minority voice in educational reform: An analysis by minority and women college of education deans.* Greenwich, CT: Ablex Publishing.

Catsambio, S. (1994). The path to math: Gender and racial-ethnic differences in mathematics participation from middle school to high school. *Sociology of Education, 67,* 199–215.

Cheney, D. L. (1993). Ethics in research: An overview. In D. L. Cheney (Ed.), *Ethical issues in research* (pp. xii–xx). Frederick, MD: University Publishing Group.

Chickering, A. W., and Ehrmann, S. C. (1996). Implementing the seven principles: Technology as lever. *AAHE Bulletin, 49*(2), 3–6.

Chickering, A. W., and Gamson, Z. (1987). Seven principles of good practice in undergraduate education. *AAHE Bulletin, 39*(7), 3–7.

Chliwniak, L. (1997). *Higher education leadership: Analyzing the gender gap* (ASHE-ERIC Higher Education Report no. 4). Washington, DC: Graduate School of Education and Human Development, George Washington University.

Cleveland, H. (1968). The dean's dilemma: Leadership of equals. In A. J. Dibden (Ed.), *The academic deanship in American colleges and universities.* Carbondale, IL: Southern Illinois University Press.

Cohen, E., and Geske, T. G. (1990). *The economics of education.* New York: Pergamon Press.

Cohen, M. C., and March, J. G. (1974). *Leadership and ambiguity: The American college president.* Boston: Harvard Business School Press.

Coladarci, A. (1980). Some notes on deans as individuals and the role of the dean. In D. E. Griffiths and D. J. McCarty (Eds.), *The dilemma of the deanship* (pp. 125–131). Danville, IL: Interstate Printers & Publishers.

Cole, J. R. (1993). Balancing acts: Dilemma of choice facing research universities. *Daedalus, 122*(4), 1–36.

Collins, J. C., and Porras, J. I. (1994). *Built to last: Successful habits of visionary companies.* New York: Harper Business.

Committee C on College and University Teaching, Research, and Publication of the American Association of University Professors. (1996). The uses of technology in college and university instruction. *Academe, 82*(3), 66–71.

Conger, J. A. (1998, May-June). The necessary art of persuasion. *Harvard Business Review,* 84–95.

Conger, J. A., and Benjamin, B. (1999). *Building leaders: How successful companies develop the next generation.* San Francisco: Jossey-Bass.

Conger, J. A., and Kanungo, R. N. (Eds.). (1988). *Charismatic leadership: The elusive factor in organizational effectiveness.* San Francisco: Jossey-Bass.

Connolly, F. W. (1994). Who are the electronic learners? Why should we worry about them? *Change, 26*(2), 39–41.

Cook, C. E., and Sorcinelli, M. D. (1999). Building multiculturalism into teaching-development programs. *AAHE Bulletin, 51*(7), 3–6.

Corson, J. J. (1960). *Governance of colleges and universities.* New York: McGraw-Hill.

Cosgrove, D. (1986). *The effects of principal succession on elementary schools.* Unpublished doctoral dissertation, University of Utah, Salt Lake City.

Costello, S. J. (1994). *Managing change in the workplace.* Burr Ridge, IL: Irwin.

Cottrell, D., and Layton, M. C. (2000). *175 ways to get more done in less time.* Dallas: Cornerstone Leadership Institute.

Coughlan, W. D. (1994). The balance of a lifetime. *Association Management, 46*(1), 66–73.

Covey, S. R. (1989). *The seven habits of highly effective people: Powerful lessons in personal change.* New York: Fireside.

Covey, S. R. (1992). *Principle-centered leadership.* New York: Simon & Schuster.

Covrig, D. M. (2000). The organizational context of moral dilemmas: The role of moral leadership in administration in making and breaking dilemmas. Quoting the remarks of the honorable Earl J. Warren at the Louis Marshall Award Dinner of the Jewish Theological Seminary of America, American Hotel, New York, 1962. *Journal of Leadership Studies, 7*(1), 40–59.

Cox, T., Jr. (1994). *Cultural diversity in organizations: Theory, research and practice.* San Francisco: Berrett-Koehler.

Cox, T., and Beale, R. (1997). *Developing competency to manage diversity: Readings, cases and activities.* San Francisco: Berrett-Koehler.

Crawford, A. L. (1983). Skills perceived to lead to success in higher education. (ED 232 519)

Creswell, J. W., and England, M. E. (1994). Improving informational resources for academic deans and chairpersons. In M. K. Kinnick (Ed.), *Providing useful information for deans and department chairs* (pp. 5–18). San Francisco: Jossey-Bass.

Cronin, B., and Crawford, H. (1999). Do deans publish what they preach? *Journal of the American Society for Information Science, 50*(5), 471–474.

Curry, L., and Wergin, J. F. (1993). *Educating professionals: Responding to new expectations for competence and accountability.* San Francisco: Jossey-Bass.

Cyphert, F. R., and Zimpher, N. L. (1980). The education deanship: Who is the dean? In D. E. Griffiths and D. J. McCarty (Eds.), *The dilemma of the deanship* (pp. 91–122). Danville, IL: Interstate Printers & Publishers.

Darling, J. R., and Pomatto, M. C. (1999). Administrative team-building in the academic institution: The key role of behavioral style. *A Leadership Journal: Women in Leadership—Sharing the Vision, 3*(2), 17–30.

Davis, N. A. (1990). Sexual harassment in the university. In S. M. Cahn (Ed.), *Morality, responsibility, and the university* (pp. 150–176). Philadelphia: Temple University Press.

Davis, R. M. (Ed.). (1985). *Leadership and institutional renewal.* San Francisco: Jossey-Bass.

Dawis, R. V. (1994). The theory of work adjustment as convergent theory. In M. L. Savickas and P. W. Lent (Eds.), *Convergence in career development theories: Implications for science and practice* (pp. 33–43). Palo Alto, CA: Consulting Psychologists.

Dawis, R. V., England, G. W., and Lofquist, L. H. (1964). *A theory of work adjustment* (Vol. 15). Minneapolis: Industrial Resource Center, University of Minnesota.

Dawis, R. V., and Lofquist, L. H. (1984). *A psychological theory of work adjustment.* Minneapolis: University of Minnesota.

Day, D. V., and Bedeian, A. G. (1995). Personality similarity and work-related outcomes among African-American nursing personnel: A test of the supplemental model of person-environment congruence. *Journal of Vocational Behavior, 46,* 55–70.

Deferrari, R. J. (Ed.). (1956). *The problems of administration in the American college.* Washington, DC: Catholic University of America Press.

DePree, M. (1992). *Leadership jazz.* New York: Dell Publishing.

Dibden, A. J. (Ed.). (1968). *The academic deanship in American colleges and universities.* Carbondale: Southern Illinois University Press.

Dill, W. R. (1980). The deanship: An unstable craft. In D. E. Griffiths and D. J. McCarty (Eds.), *The dilemma of the deanship* (pp. 261–284). Danville, IL: Interstate Printers & Publishers.

Dilts, D. A., Haber, L. J., and Bialik, D. (1994). *Assessing what professors do: An introduction to academic performance appraisal in higher education.* Westport, CT: Greenwood Press.

Doughtrey, W. H., Jr. (1991). The legal nature of academic freedom in U.S. colleges and universities. *University of Richmond Law Review, 25*(1), 233–271.

Drennan, P. (1983). The dean as administrator: Roles, functions, and attributes. *A monograph sequel: Have you ever thought of being a dean?* Washington, DC: American Association of Colleges of Nursing.

Drucker, P. F. (1967). *The effective executive.* New York: Harper & Row.

Dupont, G. E. (1968). The dean and his office. In A. J. Dibden (Ed.), *The academic deanship in American colleges and universities.* Carbondale: Southern Illinois University Press.

Dziech, B. W., and Hawkins, M. W. (1998). *Sexual harassment in higher education: Reflections and new perspectives.* New York: Garland Publishing.

Eamon, D. B. (1999). Distance education: Has technology become a threat to the academy? *Behavior, Research, Methods, Instruments, & Computers, 31*(2), 197–207.

Edwards, R. (1999). The academic department: How does it fit into the university reform agenda? *Change, 31*(5), 16–27.

Ehrlich, T. (Ed.). (2000). *Civic responsibility and higher education.* Phoenix, AZ: ACE/Oryx Press.

Ehrmann, S. C. (1994). Making sense of technology: A dean's progress. *Change, 26*(2), 34–38.

Ehrmann, S. C. (2000). Computer-intensive academic programs. *AAHE Bulletin, 53*(3), 7–11.

Elbow, P. (1981). *Writing with power.* New York: Oxford University Press.

Elliott, D. (1995). *The ethics of asking: Dilemmas in higher education fund raising.* Baltimore: Johns Hopkins University Press.

Ericsson, K. A., Krampe, R. T., and Tesch-Romer, C. (1993). The role of deliberate practices in the acquisition of expert performance. *Psychological Review, 100*(3), 363–406.

Eurich, N. P. (1990). *The learning industry: Education for adult workers*. Princeton, NJ: Carnegie Foundation for Advancement of Teaching.

Euwema, B. (1961, July). Academic tensions. *Educational Record, 42*.

Fagin, C. M. (1997). The leadership role of a dean. In M. J. Austin, F. L. Ahearn, and R. A. English (Eds.), *The professional dean: Meeting the leadership challenges* (Vol. 25). San Francisco: Jossey-Bass.

Faris, S. K. (1998). *Technology transfer as an entrepreneurial practice in higher education* (Vol. 98–9). Kansas City, MO: Kauffman Center for Entrepreneurial Leadership Clearinghouse on Entrepreneurship Education.

Feltner, B. D., and Goodsell, D. R. (1972). The academic dean and conflict management. *Journal of Higher Education, 43*(9), 692–701.

Fenstermacher, G. D. (1995). From Camelot to Chechnya: The journey of an education dean. In L. S. Bowen (Ed.), *The wizards of odds: Leadership journeys of education deans*. Washington, DC: American Association of Colleges for Teacher Education.

Finkelstein, M. J., Frances, C., Jewett, F. I., and Scholz, B. W. (Eds.). (2000). *Dollars, distance, and online education: The new economics of college teaching and learning*. Phoenix, AZ: ACE/Oryx Press.

Fisher, R., and Ury, W. (1981). *Getting to yes: Negotiating agreement without giving in*. New York: Penguin Books.

Fitzgerald, L. F. (1996). Sexual harassment: The definition and measurement of a construct. In M. A. Paludi (Ed.), *Sexual harassment on college campuses: Abusing the ivory power* (2nd ed.). Albany: State University of New York Press.

Flowers, L., Pascarella, E. T., and Pierson, C. T. (2000). Information technology use and cognitive outcomes in the first year of college. *Journal of Higher Education, 71*(6), 637–667.

Forrest, A. L. (1951, December). Some objectives and principles of academic administration. *Association of American Colleges Bulletin, 37*, 581–583.

Frances, C., Pumerantz, R., and Caplan, J. (1999). Planning for instructional technology. *Change, 31*(4), 25–33.

Friedman, S. D., Christensen, P., and DeGroot, J. (1998, November-December). Work and life: The end of the zero-sum game. *Harvard Business Review*, 119–129.

Fullan, M. (1993). *Change forces: Probing the depths of educational reform*. Philadelphia: Falmer Press.

Fullan, M. (1999). *Change forces: The sequel*. Philadelphia: Falmer Press.

Gabarro, J. J. (1985, May-June). When a new manager takes charge. *Harvard Business Review*, 110–123.

Galbo, C. (1998, May-June). Helping adults learn. *Thrust for Educational Leadership*, 13–15, 35–37.

Garcia, J.L.A. (1994). The aims of the university and the challenge of diversity: Bridging the traditionalist/multiculturalist divide. In M.N.S. Sellers (Ed.), *An ethical education: Community and morality in the multicultural university*. Providence, RI: Berg Publishers.

Gardenswartz, L., and Rowe, A. (1993). *Managing diversity: A complete desk reference and planning guide*. New York: IRWIN/Pfeiffer.

Gardner, J. W. (1990). *On leadership*. New York: Free Press.

Gardner, W. E. (1992). Once a dean: Some reflections. *Journal of Teacher Education, 43*(5), 357–366.

George, S. A., and Deets, C. (1983). Top academic nurse administrators' perceptions of essential behaviors for their positions. *Nursing Leadership, 6,* 44–55.

Gewirth, A. (1990). Human rights and academic freedom. In S. M. Cahn (Ed.), *Morality, responsibility, and the university.* Philadelphia: Temple University Press.

Gilbert, S. W. (1996). Making the most of a slow revolution. *Change, 28*(2), 10–23.

Ginzberg, E. (1959). *What makes an executive?* New York: Columbia University Press.

Gitlow, A. L. (1995). *Reflections on higher education.* Lanham, MD: University Press of America.

Gladieux, L. E., and Swail, W. S. (1999). Who will have access to the virtual university? *Change, 52*(2), 7–9.

Glazer-Raymo, J. (1999). *Shattering the myths: Women in academe.* Baltimore: Johns Hopkins University Press.

Gmelch, W. H. (1999). Building leadership capacity for institutional reform. In D. Acker (Ed.), *Leadership for higher education in agriculture.* Ames: Global Consortium of Higher Education and Research for Agriculture, Iowa State University.

Gmelch, W. H. (2000a). *The new dean: Taking charge and learning on the job.* Paper presented at the American Association of Colleges for Teacher Education Conference, Chicago, IL.

Gmelch, W. H. (2000b). *Rites of passage: Transition to the deanship.* Paper presented at the American Association of Colleges for Teacher Education Conference, Chicago, IL.

Gmelch, W. H., and Chan, W. (1994). *Thriving on stress for success.* Thousand Oaks, CA: Corwin Press.

Gmelch, W. H., and Miskin, V. D. (1993). *Strategic leadership skills for department chairs.* Boston: Anker.

Gmelch, W. H., and Miskin, V. D. (1995). *Chairing an academic department.* Newbury Park, CA: Sage Publications.

Gmelch, W. H., and Parkay, F. W. (1999). *Becoming a department chair: Negotiating the transition from scholar to administrator.* Paper presented at the Annual Meeting of the American Educational Research Association, Montreal, Quebec.

Gmelch, W. H., and Seedorf, R. (1989). Academic leadership under siege: The ambiguity and imbalance of department chairs. *Journal for Higher Education Management, 5,* 37–44.

Gmelch, W. H., Wolverton, M., and Wolverton, M. L. (1999). *The education dean's search for balance.* Paper presented at the American Association of Colleges for Teacher Education Conference, Washington, DC.

Gmelch, W. H., Wolverton, M., Wolverton, M. L., and Sarros, J. C. (1999). The academic dean: An imperiled species searching for balance. *Research in Higher Education, 40*(6), 717–740.

Goleman, D. P. (1995). *Emotional intelligence.* New York: Bantam Books.

Goleman, D. P. (1998a, November-December). What makes a leader? *Harvard Business Review,* 93–102.

Goleman, D. P. (1998b). *Working with emotional intelligence.* New York: Bantam Books.

Gorman, R. (1998). Intellectual property: The rights of faculty as creators and users. *Academe,* 23–26.

Gould, J. W. (1964). *The academic deanship*. New York: Columbia University Teachers College Press.

Grace, H. K. (1982). The dean as scholar: Clinical competence, teaching, research, and publication. *A monograph sequel: Have you ever thought of being a dean?* Washington, DC: American Association of Colleges of Nursing.

Green, K. C. (1996). The coming ubiquity of information technology. *Change, 28*(2), 24–28.

Green, K. C. (1997). Think twice—and businesslike—about distance education. *AAHE Bulletin, 50*(2), 3–6.

Green, K. C. (1999). *Summary of the 1999 campus computing survey* [Web site]. Available: http://www.campuscomputing.net/summaries/1999/index.html.

Green, M. F. (1981). Developing leadership: A paradox in academe. *New Directions in Higher Education, 9,* 11–17.

Green, M. F., and McDade, S. A. (1994). *Investing in higher education: A handbook of leadership development.* Phoenix, AZ: Oryx Press.

Griffiths, D. E., and McCarty, D. J. (Eds.). (1980). *The dilemma of the deanship.* Danville, IL: Interstate Printers & Publishers.

Grossman, E. (1981). According to Elizabeth Grossman. In American Association of Colleges of Nursing (Ed.), *The dean as administrator: Roles, functions, and attributes. A compilation of presentations from the Executive Development Series I: "Have you ever thought of being a dean?" (1980–81).* Washington, DC: American Association of Colleges of Nursing.

Guskin, A. E. (1994a, July-August). Reducing student costs and enhancing student learning: The university challenge of the 1990s. Part I: Restructuring the administration. *Change,* 23–29.

Guskin, A. E. (1994b, September-October). Reducing student costs and enhancing student learning: The university challenges of the 1990s. Part II: Restructuring the role of faculty. *Change,* pp. 16–25.

Guskin, A. E. (1996, July-August). Facing the future: The change process in restructuring universities. *Change,* pp. 26–37.

Haimann, T., and Hilgert, R. L. (1987). *Supervision: Concepts and practices of management* (4th ed.). Cincinnati: South-Western.

Hall, B. A., de Tornyay, R., and Mitsunaga, B. K. (1983). Deans in nursing: How do they see their future? *Journal of Nursing Education, 23,* 329–331.

Hall, M. R. (1993). *The dean's role in fund raising.* Baltimore: Johns Hopkins University Press.

Hallum, J. V., and Hadley, S. W. (1993). Office of scientific integrity: Why, what and how. In D. L. Cheney (Ed.), *Ethical issues in research* (pp. 31–39). Frederick, MD: University Publishing Group.

Hare, A. P., Borgatta, E. F., and Bales, R. F. (Eds.). (1955). *Small groups: Studies in social interaction.* New York: Knopf.

Hart, A. W. (1991). Leader succession and socialization: A synthesis. *Review of Educational Research, 61*(4), 451–474.

Hawken, P. L. (1981). According to Patty L. Hawken. In American Association of Colleges of Nursing (Ed.), *The dean as administrator: Roles, functions, and attributes. A compilation* of presentations from the Executive Development Series I: "Have you ever thought of being a dean?" (1980–81). Washington, DC: American Association of Colleges of Nursing.

Hawkes, H. E. (1930, May). College administration. *Journal of Higher Education, 1,* 245.

Hecht, I.W.D., Higgerson, M. L., Gmelch, W. H., and Tucker, A. (1999). *The department chair as academic leader.* Phoenix, AZ: Oryx Press.

Heck, R. H., Johnsrud, L. K., and Rosser, V. J. (1999). *Administrative effectiveness in higher education: Improving the validity and reliability of assessments.* Paper presented at the Annual Meeting of the American Educational Research Association, Montreal. Quebec.

Heenan, D. A., and Bennis, W. (1999). *Co-leaders: The power of great partnerships.* New York: Wiley.

Heifetz, R. A. (1994). *Leadership without easy answers.* Cambridge, MA: Harvard University Press.

Helgesen, S. (1990). *The female advantage: Women's ways of leadership.* New York: Doubleday/Currency.

Helgesen, S. (1995). *The web of inclusion.* New York: Doubleday/Currency.

Hendley, V. (2000). Let's talk about race: An interview with activist Angela Oh. *AAHE Bulletin, 52*(5), 7–10, 16.

Higgins, R. L. (1946). *The functions of the academic dean. Report on the answers to the questionnaires.* Paper presented at the American Conference of Academic Deans. [Place of meeting needed.]

Hilosky, A., and Watwood, B. (1997). Transformational leadership in a changing world: A survival guide for new chairs and deans. (ED 407027)

Hoenach, S. A., and Collins, E. L. (Eds.). (1990). *The economics of American universities.* Albany, New York: SUNY.

Holland, J. L. (1966). A psychological classification scheme for vocations and major fields. *Journal of Counseling Psychology, 13,* 278–288.

Hollander, E. P. (1964). *Leaders, groups, and influence.* New York: Oxford University Press.

Honeyman, D. S., and Bruhn, M. (1996). The financing of higher education. In D. S. Honeyman, J. L. Wattenbarger, and K. C. Westbrook (Eds.), *A struggle to survive: Funding higher education in the next century.* Thousand Oaks, CA: Corwin Press.

Huffman-Joley, G. (1992). *The role of the dean: Fostering teaching as scholarship in the school of education learning community.* Paper presented at the Annual Meeting of the American Association of Colleges for Teacher Education, San Antonio, TX.

Hurtado, S., Milem, J., Clayton-Pedersen, A., and Allen, W. (1999). *Enacting diverse learning environments: Improving the climate for racial/ethnic diversity in higher education* (26(8)). Washington, DC: Graduate School of Education and Human Development, George Washington University.

Hutcheson, P. A. (2000). *A professional professoriate: Unionization, bureaucratization, and the AAUP.* Nashville: Vanderbilt University Press.

Hynes, W. J. (1990). Successful proactive recruiting strategies: Quest for the best. In J. B. Bennet and D. J. Figuli (Eds.), *Enhancing departmental leadership: The roles of the chairperson.* New York: ACE/Macmillan.

Ivancevich, J. M., and Matteson, M. (1987). *Organizational behavior and management.* Plano, TX: Business Publications.

Jackson, J. (2000). *Decanal work: Using role theory and the sociology of time to study the executive behavior of college of education deans.* Unpublished doctoral dissertation, Iowa State University, Ames.

Jacobs, T. O. (1970). *Leadership and exchange in formal organizations.* Alexandria, VA: Human Resources Research Organization.

Jacobson, R. L. (1994). Wanted: Business deans. *Chronicle of Higher Education, 40*(37), A17–A18.

Johns, H. E. (1986). Effect of selected biographical factors on faculty perceptions of law school deans' leader behavior. *Higher Education, 15,* 497–506.

Johnstone, S. M., and Krauth, B. (1996). Balancing equity and access: Some principles of good practice for the virtual university. *Change, 28*(2), 38–41.

Jones, D. P. (1995). Higher education and high technology: A case for joint action. Boulder, CO: National Center for Higher Education Management Systems.

Josephson, M. S., and Hanson, W. (Eds.). (1998). *The power of character.* San Francisco: Jossey-Bass.

Kahn, R., and Byosiere, P. (1992). Stress in organizations. In M. Dunnette and L. Hough (Eds.), *Handbook of industrial and organizational psychology* (Vol. 3). Palo Alto, CA: Consulting Psychologists Press.

Kahn, R. L. (1981). *Work and health.* New York: Wiley.

Kahn, R. L., Wolfe, D. M., Quinn, R. P., and Snoek, J. D. (1964). *Organizational stress: Studies in role conflict and ambiguity.* New York: Wiley.

Kaludis, G., and Stine, G. (2000). From managing expenditures to managing costs: Strategic management for information technology. In M. J. Finkelstein, C. Frances, F. I. Jewett, and B. W. Scholz (Eds.), *Dollars, distance, and online education: The new economics of college teaching and learning* (pp. 256–268). Phoenix, AZ: ACE/Oryx Press.

Kanter, R. M. (1997). *Rosabeth Moss Kanter on the frontiers of management.* Cambridge, MA: Harvard University Press.

Kapel, D. E., and Dejnozka, E. L. (1979). The education deanship: A further analysis. *Research in Higher Education, 10,* 99–112.

Kaplan, G. R. (2000). Friends, foes, and noncombatants: Notes on public education's pressure groups. *Phi Delta Kappan, 82*(3), K1–K12.

Kaplin, W. A., and Lee, B. A. (1995). *The law of higher education: A comprehensive guide to legal implications of administrative decision making* (3rd ed.). San Francisco: Jossey-Bass.

Katz, J. H. (1989). The challenges of diversity. In C. Woolbright (Ed.), *Valuing diversity on campus: A multicultural approach* (pp. 1–21). Bloomington, IN: Association of College Unions–International.

Katzenbach, J. R. (1998). *Teams at the top: Unleashing the potential of both teams and individual leaders.* Boston: Harvard Business School Press.

Katzenbach, J. R., and Smith, D. K. (1993). *The wisdom of teams: Creating the high-performance organization.* Boston: Harvard Business School Press.

Keller, G. (1983). *Academic strategy: The management revolution in American higher education.* Baltimore: Johns Hopkins University Press.

Kellogg Commission. (1999). *Returning to our roots: A learning society.* New York: National Association of State Universities and Land-Grant Colleges.

Kellogg Foundation. (1999). *Building leadership capacity for the 21st century. A report from the Global Leadership Scan.* Battle Creek, MI: Kellogg Foundation.

Kelly, K. (1991). *Fund raising and public relations: A critical analysis.* Hillsdale, NJ: Erlbaum.

Kerr, C. (1994). Knowledge ethics and the new academic culture. *Change, 26*(1), 9–15.

Kibrick, A. (1980). *Challenges facing today's deans. The dean's role in baccalaureate and higher degree colleges of nursing.* New York: NLN Publishing.

Koch, H. C. (1968). And so you are a dean! *North Carolina Association Quarterly, 36,* 49–58.

Komives, S. R., Lucas, N., and McMahon, T. R. (1998). *Exploring leadership: For a college student who wants to make a difference.* San Francisco: Jossey-Bass.

Korn, D. (1993). Conflict of interest: A university perspective. In D. L. Cheney (Ed.), *Ethical issues in research* (pp. 113–126). Frederick, MD: University Publishing Group.

Kotter, J. (1990, May-June). What leaders really do. *Harvard Business Review,* 103–111.

Kouzes, J. M., and Posner, B. Z. (1993). *Credibility: How leaders gain and lose it, why people demand it.* San Francisco: Jossey-Bass.

Kouzes, J. M., and Posner, B. Z. (1995). *The leadership challenge: How to keep getting extraordinary things done in organizations.* San Francisco: Jossey-Bass.

Krahenbuhl, G. S. (1998). Faculty work: Integrating responsibilities and institutional needs. *Change, 30*(6), 18–25.

Kritek, P. B. (1994). *Negotiating at an uneven table: A practical approach to working with difference and diversity.* San Francisco: Jossey-Bass.

Kuh, G. D., and Whitt, E. J. (1988). *The invisible tapestry: Culture in American colleges and universities.* Washington, DC: Association for the Study of Higher Education.

Kulik, C. T., Oldham, G. R., and Hackman, J. R. (1987). Work design as an approach to person-environment fit. *Journal of Vocational Behavior, 31,* 278–296.

Lamborn, M. L. (1991). Motivation and job satisfaction of deans of schools of nursing. *Journal of Professional Nursing, 7*(1), 33–40.

Lamoreaux, D. (1990). *New shoes: An educational criticism of a new principal's first quarter.* Paper presented at the Annual Meeting of the American Educational Research Association, Boston, MA.

Lasley, T. J., and Haberman, M. (1987). How do university administrators evaluate education deans? *Journal of Teacher Education, 38*(5), 13–16.

Latta, G. F. (1996). The virtual university: Creating an emergent reality. Washington, DC: ERIC.

Lawler, E. E. (1992). *The ultimate advantage.* San Francisco: Jossey-Bass.

Lazerow, H., and Winters, J. C. (1974). In quest of a dean. *Journal of Legal Education, 26,* 59–86.

Leap, T. L. (1995). *Tenure, discrimination, and the courts* (2nd ed.). Ithaca, NY: Cornell University Press.

Leatherman, C. (Sept. 22, 2000, vol. XLVII, no. 4). Tenured professors show willingness to walk out over use of lecturers. *Chronicle of Higher Education,* A16–A17.

Levine, A., and Cureton, J. S. (1998). Collegiate life: An obituary. *Change, 30*(3), 12–17.

Levine, A. E. (2000, October 27). The future of colleges: Nine inevitable changes. *Chronicle of Higher Education,* B10–11.

Lewin, K. (1938). *The conceptual representation and the management of psychological forces.* Durham, NC: Duke University Press.

Lewis, C. T., Garcia, J. E., and Jobs, S. M. (1990). *Managerial skills in organizations.* Boston: Allyn & Bacon.

Lindberg, R. E. (1995). Seeking the elusive balance. *Association Management,* 86–92.

A little learning. (1997). *The Economist, 345*(8047), 72.

Louis, M. R. (1980). Surprise and sense making: What newcomers experience in entering unfamiliar organizational settings. *Administrative Science Quarterly, 25,* 226–251.

Lublin, J. S., and Schellhardt, T. D. (1998, April 7). The big umbrella: Travelers/Citicorp merger history shows sharing of power can lead to clashes, breakups. *Wall Street Journal,* p. C14.

Lutz, F. W. (1979). "Deanship selection and faculty governance in higher education." *Planning and Changing, 10*(4), 238–245.

Management Practice Institute. (1997). *Defining the niche for proprietary education.* Available: http://www.mpiweb.com/bull/niche.html.

Mangan, K. S. (2000, November 17). Company seeks $10 million from scientist and university. *Chronicle of Higher Education,* A49–52.

March, J. (1988). *Decisions and organizations.* New York: Blackwell.

March, J. G., and Olsen, J. P. (1979). *Ambiguity and choice in organizations* (2nd ed.). Bergen, Norway: Universitetsforlaget.

Marchese, T. (1994). What our publics want, but think they don't get, from a liberal arts education. Ted Marchese interviews Richard Hersh. *AAHE Bulletin, 47*(3), 8–10.

Marchese, T. J., and Lawrence, J. F. (1987). *The search committee handbook: A guide to recruiting administrators.* Washington, DC: American Association for Higher Education.

Marcus, L. R. (1997). Restructuring higher education governance patterns. *Review of Higher Education, 20*(4), 399–418.

Markie, P. J. (1990). Professors, students, and friendship. In S. Cahn (Ed.), *Morality, responsibility, and the university: Studies in academic ethics.* Philadelphia: Temple University Press.

Marshall, M. S. (1956). How to be a dean. *AAUP Bulletin, 42,* 636–643.

Martin, J. L. (1993). *Academic deans: An analysis of effective academic leadership at research universities.* Paper presented at the Annual Meeting of the American Educational Research Association, Atlanta, GA.

Maslen, G. (2000, November 22). Universitas 21 announces online education agreement with Thomson Learning. *Chronicle of Higher Education.*

Massy, W. F., and Wilger, A. K. (1998). "A cost-effectiveness model for the assessment of educational productivity." In J. E. Groccia and J. E. Miller (Eds.), *Enhancing productivity: Administrative, instructional, and technological strategies.* San Francisco: Jossey-Bass.

Matczynski, T., Lasky, T. J., and Haberman, M. (1989). The deanship: How faculty evaluates performance. *Journal of Teacher Education, 40*(6), 10–14.

Matusak, L. R. (1997). *Finding your voice: Learning to lead . . . anywhere you want to make a difference.* San Francisco: Jossey-Bass.

Mayhew, L. B. (1957, October). Shared responsibility of the president and the dean. *North Central Association Quarterly, 32,* 191.

McAdams, R. P. (1997). Revitalizing the department chair: Ten recommendations to make the role more attractive, powerful, and effective. *AAHE Bulletin, 49*(6), 10–13.

McBride, S. A. (2000). Academic economics: The academic dean and financial management, *New Directions for Community Colleges* (pp. 51–62). San Francisco: Jossey-Bass.

McCaskey, M. (1979, November-December). The hidden messages managers send. *Harvard Business Review,* 135–148.

McGeehan, P. (1997, December 2). Charles Schwab's Pottruck will share title of CEO with company's founder. *Wall Street Journal,* p. B5.

McGinnis, A. (1933). The dean and his duties. *Journal of Higher Education, 4,* 193.

McGrath, E. J. (1936, 1999). The dean. *Journal of Higher Education, 70*(5), 599–605.

McGrath, E. J. (1947). The office of the academic dean. In N. Burns (Ed.), *The administration of higher institutions under changing conditions.* Chicago: University of Chicago Press.

McGregor, D. M. (1960). *The human side of enterprise.* New York: McGraw-Hill.

McHugh, W. F. (1973). Faculty unionism and tenure. *Journal of College and University Law, 1*(1), 46–74.

Meisinger, R. J., Jr. (1994). *College and university budgeting: An introduction for faculty and academic administrators.* Washington, DC: National Association of College and University Business Officers.

Mercer, J. (1997). Fund raising has become a job requirement for many deans. *Chronicle of Higher Education, 45*(45), A31–A32.

Merisotis, J. P., and Phipps, R. A. (1999). What's the difference? Outcomes of distance vs. traditional classroom-based learning. *Change, 31*(3), 13–17.

Merz, C. (1999). *Understanding the organization: Frames and models.* Paper presented at the Annual Meeting of the American Association of Colleges for Teacher Education, Washington, DC.

Metz, P. (1995). The view from a university library. *Change, 27*(1), 29–33.

Miller, P. M. (1989). A study of professional characteristics of deans of colleges of business. *Higher Education Management, 1*(2), 107–115.

Miller, R. I. (1974). The academic dean. *Intellect, 102,* 231–234.

Milner, C. A. (1936). *The dean of the small college.* Boston: Christopher Publishing House.

Minnick, W. C. (1968). *The art of persuasion.* Boston: Houghton Mifflin.

Mintzberg, H. (1973). *The nature of managerial work.* New York: Harper & Row.

Mintzberg, H. (1989). *Mintzberg on management: Inside our strange world of organizations.* New York: Free Press.

Mintzberg, H. (1998, November-December). Covert leadership: Notes on managing professionals. *Harvard Business Review,* 140–147.

Mitgang, L. (1996). A nation of architectural illiterates? *AAHE Bulletin, 49*(2), 7–9.

Monat, A., and Lazarus, R. S. (1977). *Stress and coping: An anthology.* New York: Columbia University Press.

Moore, K. M. (1982). *Women and minorities. Leaders in transition: A national study of higher education administrators.* New York: Exxon Education & Ford Foundation.

Morgan, G. (1980). Paradigms, metaphors, and puzzle solving in organizational theory. *Administrative Science Quarterly, 16,* 607–622.

Morris, V. C. (1981). *Deaning: Middle management in academe.* Urbana: University of Illinois Press.

Morrison, A. M. (1992). *The new leaders: Guidelines on leadership diversity in America.* San Francisco: Jossey-Bass.

Morsink, C. (1987). Critical functions of educational administrators: Perception of deans and chairs. *Journal of Teacher Education, 38*(5), 23–27.

Mortenson, T. G. (1994a, September). Part-time college enrollment: It's mostly a matter of age. *Postsecondary Education Opportunity, 27,* 1–19.

Mortenson, T. G. (1994b, October). Raising tuition . . . to build prisons: Infatuation with incarceration. *Postsecondary Education Opportunity, 28,* 7–13.

Mortenson, T. G. (1994c, January). Whose responsibility is it? Shifting responsibilities for financing higher education from government to individuals. *Postsecondary Education Opportunity, 19,* 7–16.

Murdock, S. H., and Hoque, M. N. (1999). Demographic factors affecting higher education in the U.S. in the twenty-first century. *New Directions for Higher Education, 108* (Winter), 5–13.

Murray, B. (2000). Reinventing class discussion on-line. *Monitor on Psychology, 31*(4), 54–56.

Newton, N. (1985). Letter to a search and screen committee for a dean of liberal arts. *Liberal Education, 71*(4), 295–303.

Nies, C. T., and Wolverton, M. (2000). *Mentoring deans.* Paper presented at the Annual Meeting of the American Educational Research Association, New Orleans, LA.

Noam, E. (1995). Electronics and the dim future of the university. *Science, 270,* 247–249.

North, J. D. (1995). "Read my lips": The academic administrator's role in the campus focus on teaching. *AAHE Bulletin, 48*(2), 3–6.

Oakes, J. L. (1999). Women as capable leaders in higher education administration: A historical journey with implications for professional mentoring. *A Leadership Journal: Women in Leadership—Sharing the Vision, 3*(2), 57–62.

O'Connor, P. (2000). *When words fail me: What everyone who writes should know about writing.* New York: Harvest Books.

Olivas, M. A. (1997). *The law and higher education.* Durham, NC: Carolina Academic Press.

Olswang, S. G., and Fantel, J. I. (1980). Tenure and periodic performance review: Compatible legal and administrative principles. *Journal of College and University Law, 7*(1), 1–30.

Oncken W., Jr., and Wass, D. L. (1974). Management time—Who's got the monkey? *Harvard Business Review, 52*(6), 75.

Oncken, W., Jr., Wass, D. L., and Covey, S. R. (1999, November-December). Management time: Who's got the monkey? *Harvard Business Review,* 179–186.

O'Neil, H. F., Jr., Bensimon, E. M., Diamond, M. A., and Moore, M. R. (1999). Designing and implementing an academic scorecard. *Change, 31*(6), 32–40.

O'Reilly, B. (1994, August 8). What's killing the business school deans of America? *Fortune,* 64–68.

Ost, D. H., and Twale, D. J. (1989). Appointment of administrators in higher education: Reflections of administrative structures and organizational structures. *Initiatives, 52*(2), 23–30.

Ostroff, F. (1999). *The horizontal organization: What the organization of the future looks like and how it delivers value to customers.* New York: Oxford University Press.

Otis, J., and Caragonne, P. (1979). Factors in the resignation of graduate school of social work deans. *Journal of Education for Social Work, 19,* 59–64.

O'Toole, J. (1995). *Leading change.* San Francisco: Jossey-Bass.

Paludi, M. A. (Ed.). (1990). *Ivory power: Sexual harassment on campus.* Albany: State University of New York.

Paludi, M. A. (Ed.). (1996). *Sexual harassment on college campuses: Abusing the ivory power* (2nd ed.). Albany: State University of New York Press.

Paludi, M. A., and Barickman, R. B. (1998). *Sexual harassment, work, and education: A resource manual for prevention* (2nd ed.). Albany: State University of New York Press.

Paretsky, J. M. (1993). Judicial review of discretionary grants of higher education tenure. *Education Law Reporter, 83,* 17–26.

Parkay, F. W., and Hall, G. E. (1992). *Becoming a principal: The challenges of beginning leadership.* Boston: Allyn & Bacon.

Parker, G. M. (1996). *Team players and teamwork: The new competitive business strategy.* San Francisco: Jossey-Bass.

Parkhurst, W. (1988). *The eloquent executive.* New York: Times Books.

Parsons, T. and Platt, G. M. (1973). *The American university.* Cambridge, MA: Harvard University Press.

Peer review. (1999, November 26). *Chronicle of Higher Education,* A14.

Penslar, R. L. (1995). *Research ethics: Cases and materials.* Bloomington: Indiana University Press.

Perelman, L. (1993). *School's out: Hyperlearning, the new technology, and the end of education.* New York: Knopf.

Peters, T., and Waterman, R. J. (1982). *In search of excellence: Lessons from America's best-run companies.* New York: Warner Books.

Pfeffer, J., and Viega, J. (1999). Putting people first for organizational success. *Academy of Management Executive, 13*(2), 37–48.

Phillips, E. C., Morrell, C., and Chronister, J. L. (1996). Responses to reduced state funding. *New Directions for Higher Education, 94,* 9–20.

Phillips, R. C. (1969). Selecting the academic dean. *Educational Record, 50*(1), 66–70.

Poch, S., and Wolverton, M. (2000). *The nexus between academic deans and corporate CEOs: An opportunity in the making.* Paper presented at the Annual Meeting of the American Educational Research Association, New Orleans, LA.

Pollock, D. (1998). *The transition experience in international settings.* Shanghai, China: East Asia Regional Conference for Overseas Schools.

Poskzim, P. S. (1984, October). New administrators: A statistical look at movement within the ranks, 1982–83. *Change,* 55–59.

Pratt, C. D. (1999). In the wake of *Hopwood:* An update on affirmative action in the education arena. *Howard Law Journal, 42,* 451–467.

Press, E., and Washburn, J. (2000). The kept university. *Atlantic Monthly, 283*(2), 39–54.

Privateer, P. M. (1999). Academic technology and the future of higher education: Strategic paths taken and not taken. *Journal of Higher Education, 70*(1), 60–79.

Prock, V. N. (1981). According to Valencia N. Prock. In American Association of Colleges of Nursing (Ed.), *The dean as administrator: Roles, functions, and attributes. A compilation of presentations from the Executive Development Series I: "Have you ever thought of being a dean?" (1980–81)*. Washington, DC: American Association of Colleges of Nursing.

Prock, V. N. (1983). The dean as a person: Rights and responsibilities. *A monograph sequel: Have you ever thought of being a dean?* Washington, DC: American Association of Colleges of Nursing.

Promising Practices Team of the President's Initiative on Race. (1999). *Pathways to one America in the 21st century: Promising practices for racial reconciliation*. Washington, DC: President's Initiative on Race.

Pumerantz, R., and Frances, C. (2000). Wide-angle view of the costs of introducing new technologies to the instructional program. In M. J. Finkelstein, C. Frances, F. I. Jewett, and B. W. Scholz (Eds.), *Dollars, distance, and online education: The new economics of college teaching and learning* (pp. 241–255). Phoenix, AZ: ACE/Oryx Press.

Putnam, R. (1995). Bowling alone: America's declining social capital. *Journal of Democracy, 6*(1), p. 65.

Rachels, J. (1993). Are quotas sometimes justified? In S. Cahn (Ed.), *Affirmative action and the university: A philosophical inquiry* (pp. 217–222). Philadelphia: Temple University Press.

Ramaley, J. A. (2000). Embracing civic responsibility. *AAHE Bulletin, 52*(7), 9–13, 20.

Regan, H. B., and Brooks, G. H. (1995). *Out of women's experience: Creating relational leadership*. Thousand Oaks, CA: Corwin Press.

Reid, J. Y., and Rogers, S. J. (1981). *The search for academic leadership: Selecting chief academic officers in American colleges and universities*. Paper presented at the ASHE Annual Meeting in Washington, D.C.

Richardson, R. C., Jr., and Skinner, E. F. (1991). *Achieving quality and diversity: Universities in a multicultural society*. New York: ACE/Macmillan.

Riggs, R. O., Murrell, P. H., and Cutting, J. C. (1993). *Sexual harassment in higher education: From conflict to community*. Washington, DC: School of Education and Human Development, George Washington University.

Rizzo, J. R., House, R. J., and Lirtzman, S. I. (1970). Role conflict and ambiguity in complex organizations. *Administrative Science Quarterly, 15,* 150–163.

Robbins, J. H., Schmitt, D. M., Ehinger, M., and Welliver, M. (1994). *Who is leading us toward quality professional development?* Paper presented at the Convention of the American Association of Colleges of Teacher Education, Chicago, IL.

Rockhurst College Continuing Education Center. (1995a). *Self-profile: A guide for positive interpersonal communication*. Shawnee Mission, KS: National Press Publications.

Rockhurst College Continuing Education Center. (1995b). *The stress management handbook: A practical guide to reducing stress in every aspect of your life*. Shawnee Mission, KS: National Press Publications.

Rockhurst College Continuing Education Center. (1997). *Powerful communication skills: How to communicate with confidence, clarity and credibility*. Shawnee Mission, KS: National Press Publications.

Rosenheim, E., Jr. (1963, September). Letter to a new dean. *Bulletin of the American Association of University Professors, 49*.

Rosovsky, H. (1990). *The university: An owner's manual.* New York: Norton.

Rossbacher, L. A. (1999). Harassment. In G. Allan (Ed.), *Resource handbook for academic deans* (pp. 116–117). Washington, DC: American Conference of Academic Deans.

Rost, J. C. (1993). *Leadership for the twenty-first century.* Westport, CT: Praeger.

Russell, T. (1998). *The "no significant difference" phenomenon.* Available: http:/teleeducation.nb.ca/phenom/.

Russo, C. J. (Ed.). (1999). *The yearbook of education law, 1999.* Dayton, OH: Education Law Association.

Ryan, D. (1980). Deans as individuals in organizations. In D. Griffith and D. McCarty (Eds.), *The dilemma of the deanship.* Danville, IL: Interstate Printers & Publishers.

Sarros, J. C., and Gmelch, W. H. (1996). *The role of the department head in Australian universities.* Melbourne, Australia: Monash University.

Schatzberg, K. (1999). Physical disabilities and learning disabilities. In G. Allan (Ed.), *Resource handbook for academic deans.* Washington, DC: American Conference of Academic Deans.

Schein, E. (1992). *Organizational culture and leadership,* (2nd ed.). San Francisco: Jossey-Bass.

Schuh, J. H. (1974). *The role of the dean of the liberal arts college in academic administration.* Unpublished doctoral dissertation, Arizona State University, Tempe, AZ.

Schuler, R. S. (1984). Organizational stress and coping: A model and overview. In A. S. Sethi and R. S. Schuler (Eds.), *Handbook of organizational stress and coping strategies* (pp. 35–68). Cambridge, MA: Ballinger.

Schwadel, F. (1991, May 21). Nordstrom taps four nonfamily members for newly created post of copresident. *Wall Street Journal,* p. C9.

Scott, D. K., and Awbrey, S. M. (1993). Transforming scholarship. *Change, 25*(4), 38–43.

Scott, M. M. (1998). Intellectual property rights: A ticking time bomb in academia. *Academe, 84*(3), 22–26.

Scott, R. A. (1978). *Lords, squires, and yeomen: Collegiate middle managers and their organizations* (Research Report 7). Washington, DC: American Association for Higher Education.

Scott, R. A. (1979). The "amateur dean" in a complex university: An essay on role ambiguity. *Liberal Education, 65*(4), 445–452.

Scott, R. A. (1993). Are you managing your time or is time managing you? *Supervision, 54*(11), 14–18.

Seedorf, R. (1990). *Transition to leadership: The university department chair.* Unpublished doctoral dissertation, Washington State University, Pullman, WA.

Seldin, P. (1988). *Evaluating and developing administrative performance: A practical guide for academic leaders.* San Francisco: Jossey-Bass.

Senge, P. (1990). *The fifth discipline: The art and practice of the learning organization.* New York: Doubleday/Currency.

Sessa, V. I., and Taylor, J. J. (2000). *Executive selection: Strategies for success.* San Francisco: Jossey-Bass and Center for Creative Leadership.

Sherman, S. (1995, December). Wanted: Company change agents. *Fortune, 11,* 197–198.

Singleton, S. E., Burack, C. A., and Hirsch, D. J. (1997). Faculty service enclaves. *AAHE Bulletin, 49*(8), 3–7.

Sink, D. W., Jr., and Jackson, K. L. (2000). Bridging the digital divide: A collaborative approach. *Community College Journal, 71*(2), 38–41.

Smith, G. T. (1977). The development program. In W. Rowland (Ed.), *Handbook of institutional advancement: A practical guide to college and university relations, fund raising, alumni, government relations, publications, and executive management for continued advancement.* San Francisco: Jossey-Bass.

Smith, S. C., and Piele, P. K. (Eds.). (1997). *School leadership: Handbook for excellence.* Eugene: University of Oregon, ERIC Clearinghouse on Educational Management.

Socolow, D. J. (1978, May). How administrators get their jobs. *Change, 10,* 42–43, 54.

Soley, L. C. (1995). *Leasing the ivory tower: The corporate takeover of academia.* Boston: South End Press.

Sorenson, G. J. (2000). Taking robes off: When leaders step down. In B. Kellerman and L. R. Matusak (Eds.), *Cutting edge: Leadership 2000.* College Park, MD: Center for the Advanced Study of Leadership.

Sperling, J., and Tucker, R. W. (1997). *For-profit higher education: Developing a world-class workforce.* New Brunswick, NJ: Transaction Publishing.

Spero, J. R. (1983). Challenges for nursing administrators. *A monograph sequel: Have you ever thought of being a dean?* Washington, DC: American Association of Colleges of Nursing.

Spurgeon, D. (2000, September 8). In return to power, the Nordstrom family finds a pile of problems: A father and son must chart new course after a fling with halters and hip-hop. *Wall Street Journal,* p. B1.

Stage, F. K., and Manning, K. (1992). Enhancing the multicultural campus environment: A cultural brokering approach. In M. J. Barr and M. L. Upcraft (Eds.), *New Directions for Student Services* (Vol. 60). San Francisco: Jossey-Bass.

Stanton, T. H. (1990). *Maintaining the federal government's commitment to education: The case for preserving the deduction for state and local income and property taxes.* Washington, DC: ERIC. (ED 328 948)

Stark, J., Lowther, M., and Hagerty, B. (1986). *Responsive professional education: Balancing outcomes and opportunities* (ASHE-ERIC Higher Education Report 3). Washington, DC: Association for the Study of Higher Education.

Steil, L., Baker, L. L., and Watson, K. W. (1983). *Effective listening.* Reading, MA: Addison-Wesley.

Stein, R. H., and Trachtenberg, S. J. (Eds.). (1993). *The art of hiring in America's colleges & universities.* Buffalo, NY: Prometheus Books.

Stevens, E. (1999). *Due process and higher education: A systemic approach to fair decision making.* (ASHE-ERIC Higher Education Report 27(2)). Washington, DC: Graduate School of Education and Human Development, George Washington University.

Straton-Spicer, A. Q., and Spicer, C. H. (1987). Socialization of the academic chairperson: A typology of communication dimensions. *Educational Administration Quarterly, 23*(1), 41–64.

Strope, J. L., Jr. (1999). Academic freedom: In our minds, the legal myth dies slowly! *NASSP Bulletin, 83*(610), 14–21.

Strunk, W., Jr., and White, E. B. (1979). *The elements of style* (3rd ed.). Needham Heights, MA: Allyn & Bacon.

Sturtevant, W. T. (1997). *The artful journey: Cultivating and soliciting the major gift.* Chicago: Bonus Books.

Swazey, J. P., Lewis, K. S., and Anderson, M. S. (1994, March 9). The ethical training of graduate students requires serious and continuing attention. *Chronicle of Higher Education,* B1–B2.

Tatum, B. D. (1992). Talking about race, learning about racism: The application of racial identity development theory in the classroom. *Harvard Educational Review, 62*(1), 1–24.

Taylor, B. E., and Massy, W. F. (1996). *Strategic indicators for higher education, 1996.* Princeton, NJ: Peterson's.

Tell, C. (2000). The I-generation: From toddlers to teenagers, A conversation with Jan M. Healy. *Educational Leadership, 58*(2), 8–13.

Thiessen, D., and Howey, K. R. (Eds.). (1998). *Agents, provocateurs: Reform-minded leaders for schools of education.* Washington, DC: American Association of Colleges for Teacher Education.

Thompson, G. (2000). Unfulfilled prophecy: The evolution of corporate colleges. *Journal of Higher Education, 71*(3), 322–341.

Tierney, W. G. (Ed.). (1998). *The responsive university: Restructuring for high performance.* Baltimore: Johns Hopkins University Press.

Toma, J. D., and Palm, R. L. (1999). *The academic administrator and the law: What every dean and department chair needs to know* (Vol. 26, no. 5). Washington, DC: Graduate School of Education and Human Development, George Washington University.

Touchton, J., and Davis, L. (1991). *Fact book on women in higher education.* New York: Macmillan.

Townsend, B. K., and Bassoppo-Moyo, S. (1996). *If I'd only known: Administrative preparation that could have made a difference.* Paper presented at the Annual Meeting of the American Educational Research Association, New York, NY.

Tracy, S. (1986). Finding the right person—and collegiality. *College Teaching, 34*(2), 59–62.

Tucker, A., and Bryan, R. A. (1988). *The academic dean: Dove, dragon and diplomat.* New York: Macmillan.

Twale, D. J. (1997). Women in the deanship: Quest for academic deanship. *A Leadership Journal: Women in Leadership—Sharing the Vision, 1*(2), 71–80.

Twombly, S. B. (1992). The process of choosing a dean. *Journal of Higher Education, 63*(6), 653–683.

U.S. General Accounting Office. (1998). *Technology transfer: Administration of the Bayh-Dole Act by research universities* (Report to Congressional Committees GAO/RCED-98–126). Washington, DC: U.S. General Accounting Office.

University of Phoenix. (1999). *Home page.* Available: http://www.uophx.edu.

Ury, W. (1993). *Getting past no: Negotiating your way from confrontation to cooperation.* New York: Bantam Books.

Van Alstyne, C., and Withers, J. S. (1977). *Women and minorities in administration of education institutions: Employment patterns and salary comparisons.* Washington, DC: College and University Personnel Association.

Van Dusen, G. C. (1997). *The virtual campus: Technology and reform in higher education* (ASHE-ERIC Higher Education Report 25(5)). Washington, DC: George Washington University.

Van Dusen, G. C. (2000). *Digital dilemma: Issues of access, cost, and quality in media-enhanced and distance education* (ASHE-ERIC Higher Education Report 27(5)). San Francisco: Jossey-Bass.

Vandament, W. E. (1989). *Managing money in higher education: A guide to the financial process and effective participation within it.* San Francisco: Jossey-Bass.

Wagner DeCew, J. (1990). Free speech on campus. In S. M. Cahn (Ed.), *Morality, responsibility, and the university* (pp. 32–55). Philadelphia: Temple University Press.

Walvoord, B. E., and others. (2000). Academic departments: How they work, how they change. *ASHE-ERIC Higher Education Report 27*(8). San Francisco: Jossey-Bass.

Wang, A. Y., and Newlin, M. H. (2000). Characteristics of students who enroll and succeed in psychology Web-based classes. *Journal of Educational Psychology, 92*(1), pp. 137–143.

Ward, M. S. (1934). *Philosophies of administration current in the deanship of the liberal arts college.* New York: Bureau of Publications, Teachers College, Columbia University.

Watkins, B. (1999). Affirmative action/equal opportunity. In G. Allan (Ed.), *Resource handbook for academic deans* (pp. 109–112). Washington, DC: American Conference of Academic Deans.

Watson, G., and Johnson, D. (1972). *Social psychology: Issues and insights.* Philadelphia: Lippincott.

Watts, B. (1996). Legal issues. In M. A. Paludi (Ed.), *Sexual harassment on college campuses: Abusing the ivory power* (pp. 1–2). Albany: State University of New York Press.

Weeks, K. M. (1982). *Legal deskbook for administrators of independent colleges and universities.* Notre Dame, IN: Center for Constitutional Studies, Notre Dame Law School.

Weindling, D., and Early, P. (1987). *Secondary leadership: The first years.* Philadelphia: NFER-Nelson.

Welsh, J. F. (2000). Course ownership in a new technological context: The dynamics of problem definition. *Journal of Higher Education, 71*(6), 668–699.

West, C. (1993). *Race matters.* New York: Vintage Books.

Wheatley, M. J. (1992). *Leadership and the new science: Learning about organization from an orderly universe.* San Francisco: Berrett-Koehler.

Whicker, M. L., and Kronenfeld, J. J. (1994). *Dealing with ethical dilemmas on campus.* Thousand Oaks, CA: Sage Publications.

Whitt, E. J., and others. (1997). Interactions with peers and objective self-reported cognitive outcome across three years of college. *Journal of College Student Development, 40*(1), pp. 61–78.

Wightman, L. F. (1997). The threat to diversity in legal education: An empirical analysis of the consequences of abandoning race as a factor in law school admission decisions. *NYU Law Review, 72*, 1–53.

Wilcox, J. R., and Ebbs, S. L. (1992). *The leadership compass: Values and ethics in higher education* (ASHE-ERIC Higher Education Report no. 1). Washington, DC: George Washington University.

Winston, G. C. (1994). The decline in undergraduate teaching: Moral failure or market pressure? *Change, 26*(5), 8–15.

Wisniewski, R. (1998). The new Sisyphus: The dean as change agent. In D. Thiessen and K. R. Howey (Eds.), *Agents, provocateurs: Reform-minded leaders for schools of education.* Washington, DC: American Association of Colleges for Teacher Education.

Wolfe, C. R. (2001). Learning and teaching on the World Wide Web. In C. R. Wolfe (Ed.), *Learning and teaching on the World Wide Web.* San Diego: Academic Press.

Wolverton, M. (1998a, Spring). Champions of change, change agents and collaborators in change: Leadership keys to successful systemic change. *Journal of Higher Education Policy & Management, 20*(1), 19–30.

Wolverton, M. (1998b). The road to the academic deanship begins at home. *Center for Academic Leadership Newsletter, 6*(1), 1–4.

Wolverton, M., Gmelch, W. H., and Sorenson, D. (1998). The department as double agent: The call for departmental change and renewal. *Innovative Higher Education, 22*(3), 203–215.

Wolverton, M., Gmelch, W. H., and Wolverton, M. L. (2000). Finding a better person-environment fit in the academic deanship. *Innovative Higher Education, 24*(3), 203–226.

Wolverton, M., Gmelch, W. H., Wolverton, M. L., and Sarros, J. C. (1999). Stress in academic leadership: U.S. and Australian department chairs/heads. *The Review of Higher Education, 22*(2), 165–185.

Wolverton, M., and Gonzales, M. J. (2000). *Career paths of academic deans.* Paper presented at the Annual Meeting of the American Educational Research Association, New Orleans, LA.

Wolverton, M., Montez, J., and Gmelch, W. H. (2000). *The roles and challenges of deans.* Paper presented at the Annual Meeting if the Association for the Study of Higher Education, Sacramento, CA.

Wolverton, M., Wolverton, M. L., and Gmelch, W. H. (1999). The impact of role conflict and ambiguity on academic deans. *Journal of Higher Education, 70*(1), 80–106.

Wolverton, M. L., and Wolverton, M. (1999). Toward a common perception of ethical behavior in real estate. In S. E. Roulac (Ed.), *Ethics in real estate.* Norwell, MA: Kluwer Academic Publishers.

Woodburne, L. S. (1950). *Faculty personnel policies in higher education.* New York: Harper & Row.

Woolf, P. K. (1993). Distinguishing between error and fraud in science. In D. L. Cheney (Ed.), *Ethical issues in research* (pp. 3–14). Frederick, MD: University Publishing Group.

Yarger, S. J. (1998). Addressing the dean's dilemma. In D. Thiessen and K. R. Howey (Eds.), *Agents, provocateurs: Reform-minded leaders for schools of education.* Washington, DC: American Association of Colleges for Teacher Education.

Yingling, D. B. (1981). According to Doris B. Yingling. In American Association of Colleges of Nursing (Ed.), *The dean as administrator: Roles, functions, and attributes. A compilation of presentations from the Executive Development Series I: "Have you ever thought of being a dean?" (1980–1981).* Washington, DC: American Association of Colleges of Nursing.

Yukl, G. (1998). *Leadership in organizations* (4th ed.). Upper Saddle River, NJ: Prentice-Hall.

Zamson, G. (2000). Afterword. In T. Ehrlich (Ed.), *Civic responsibility and higher education.* Phoenix, AZ: ACE/Oryx Press.

Zemsky, R., and Wagner, G. R. (1997). Shaping the future. In P. M. Callan and J. E. Finney (Eds.), *Public and private financing of higher education: Shaping public policy for the future* (pp. 60–73). Phoenix, AZ: ACE/Oryx Press.

Zimpher, N. L. (1995). What deans do: A reflection on reflections. In L. S. Bowen (Ed.), *The wizards of odds: Leadership journeys of education deans.* Washington, DC: American Association of Colleges for Teacher Education.

Name Index

Abramson, L. W., 3, 7, 10, 25, 27
Ahearn, F. L., 1, 2, 3, 5, 9, 13, 50
Albert, L. S., 86, 90
Allen, C., 31
Allen, W., 54, 57
Allen-Meares, P., 1
Alstete, J. W., 88
Amabile, T. M., 44
Andersen, D. A., 3, 7, 96
Anderson, M. S., 67
Arends, R., 2, 49
Astin, A. W., 33, 36, 44
Astin, H. S., 44, 86
Austin, A. E., 1, 20, 100, 104, 108
Austin, M. J., 1, 2, 3, 5, 9, 13, 50
Avolio, B., 42
Awbrey, S. M., 36

Baez, B., 119
Baker, L. L., 102
Baker, W. J., 32
Bales, R. F., 42
Banks, J. A., 51
Bardaracco, J. S., Jr., 69
Barickman, R. B., 62, 63
Barker, D. I., 31
Barker, S. L., 102
Barnard, J., 32
Barzun, J. M., 2
Bass, B. M., 42, 43, 44
Bass, R., 31, 37, 70, 72, 87
Bassoppo-Moyo, S., 3, 25, 32, 78, 80

Bateson, M. C., 108
Batson, T., 31, 37, 70, 72, 87
Bauer, R. C., 24
Bedeian, A. G., 22
Belenky, M. F., 44
Benjamin, B., 101
Bennis, W. G., 42, 43, 47, 50, 69, 103
Bensimon, E. M., 19, 42, 43, 45, 89, 91
Bergquist, W. H., 19, 20, 46
Birnbaum, R., 11, 19, 42, 43, 89, 96
Blum, A. A., 12, 96, 97
Boettcher, J. V., 73, 74, 78
Bogue, E. G., 69
Bok, D., 86, 87
Borgatta, E. F., 42
Bowen, H. R., 75
Bower, F., 11
Bowker, L. H., 3, 7, 21, 23
Boyer, E., 67, 92
Bradford, D. L., 44
Brewer, K. C., 22
Brittingham, B. E., 80, 81
Bronstein, P., 8
Brooks, G. H., 43, 44
Brown, J. S., 35, 38, 70
Brubacher, J. S., 5
Bruhn, M., 75
Bryan, R. A., 3, 12, 14, 16, 18, 89, 101
Burgos-Sasscer, R., 36
Burns, J. M., 42, 43, 69
Byosiere, P., 22

Frances, C., 28, 31, 34, 78
Friedman, S. D., 38, 85, 107
Fullan, M., 46, 47, 48
Gabarro, J. J., 98, 103
Galbo, C., 101
Gamson, Z., 70
Garcia, J. E., 22, 67, 83
Gardenswartz, L., 52, 54, 55, 56, 57
Gardner, J. W., 69
Gardner, W. E., 17
George, S. A., 24
Geske, T. G., 29
Gewirth, A., 68
Gilbert, S. W., 71, 72, 73
Ginzberg, E., 14, 19
Gitlow, A. L., 80, 81
Gladieux, L. E., 75
Gloster, A., II, 32
Gmelch, W. H., 2, 5, 7, 8, 9, 11, 16, 20, 21, 22, 23, 24, 32, 38, 39, 40, 82, 84, 89, 90, 95, 98, 99, 100, 103, 104, 107, 108
Goldberger, N. R., 44
Goleman, D. P., 43
Gonzales, M. J., 11, 104
Goodsell, D. R., 15
Gorman, R., 73
Gould, J. W., 2, 3, 6, 10, 11, 14, 15, 18, 21, 22, 23, 24, 27, 100, 104
Grace, H. K., 17, 40, 85
Green, K. C., 32, 37, 38, 70, 71, 72, 74, 75
Green, M. F., 100, 101
Griffiths, D. E., 5, 6, 7, 11, 12, 25
Grossman, E., 12, 15, 100, 102, 105
Guskin, A. E., 46, 47, 48, 49

Haberman, M., 45, 105
Hackman, J. R., 22
Hadley, S. W., 68
Hagerty, B., 32
Haimann, T., 76
Hall, B. A., 24
Hall, G. E., 99
Hall, M. R., 17, 80, 81
Hallum, J. V., 68
Hanson, W., 69
Hard, K., 47, 48
Hare, A. P., 42

Hart, A. W., 98
Hawken, P. L., 15
Hawkes, H. E., 13
Hawkins, M. W., 62, 63, 64
Hecht, I.W.D., 102
Heck, R. H., 105
Heenan, D. A., 103
Heifetz, R. A., 42, 43
Helgesen, S., 43, 44
Hendley, V., 51, 52
Higgerson, M. L., 102
Higgins, R. L., 13
Hilgert, R. L., 76
Hilosky, A., 46, 48
Holland, J. L., 22
Hollander, E. P., 42
Honeyman, D. S., 75
House, R. J., 21
Howey, K. R., 1, 3, 12, 25
Huffman-Joley, G., 45, 46
Hurtado, S., 54, 57
Hutcheson, P. A., 65
Hutchins, R., 69
Hynes, W. J., 95

Ivancevich, J. M., 22, 84

Jackson, J., 100, 101
Jackson, K. L., 71
Jacobs, T. O., 42
Jacobson, R. L., 29
Jobs, S. M., 22, 83
Johns, H. E., 8, 9
Johnson, D., 46
Johnstone, S. M., 33, 34, 71, 74
Johnstrud, L. K., 105
Jones, D. P., 71
Josephson, M. S., 69

Kahn, R. L., 22
Kaludis, G., 74, 78
Kanter, R. M., 44
Kanungo, R. N., 42
Kapel, D. E., 21
Kaplan, W. A., 31
Kaplin, W. A., 58, 59, 60, 64, 66
Katz, J. H., 56

Subject Index

Charles Schwab Corp., 107

Chronicle of Higher Education, 12, 69, 78, 96

Civil Rights Act (1964), 60, 62

Collaboration: connectiveness results from, 44; emotional intelligence to develop, 43

Colleges: budgeting process for, 78–79; dean evaluation by, 104–106; nurturing integrity of, 86–87; reconnection with community by, 90–92; rethinking dean position by, 106–108; selection of deans for, 11–13, 95–98. *See also* Institutions; Universities

Commercially sponsored research, 30

Committee C., 33

Community reconnection, 90–92

Council of Colleges of Arts and Sciences, 101

Culture: academic, 19; dean role in creating diverse, 51–58; institution, 19–20; promoting proper hiring, 61

Curricular reform: relevance demands and, 30–31; technical advancements and, 32–33

Dean challenges: curricular relevance demands as, 30; faculty-student-system incongruence as, 35–38; fiscal constraints/accountability as, 28–30; issues of balance as, 38–41, 82–86; shifting student demographics as, 34–35; technical advancements/educational delivery systems as, 32–34; unique nature of, 27–28

Dean mentorships, 99

Dean preparation: state of current, 25–26; suggestions for, 24–25

Dean selection: current process of, 95–98; history of, 11–13

Dean socialization, 98–100

Dean strategies: for academic freedom promotion, 64–65; antidiscrimination in practice as, 58–62; for becoming technologically connected, 70; for boundary management, 84–85; for contractual relationship with faculty, 65–66; for contractual relationship with students, 66–67; creating diverse culture as, 51–58; for dealing with sexual harassment, 62–64; for efficient use of fiscal resources, 73–75; for enhancing student learning/education delivery, 70–72; for finding balance, 82–86; for fiscal management, 75–79; knowing legal environment as, 58; listing specific, 50–51; for nurturing college integrity, 86–94; for personnel productivity, 72–73; for promoting ethic practice, 67–69, 86–87; for reconnecting with community, 90–92; for redefining faculty work, 87–88; for refocusing department chairs, 89–90; for reframing academic departments, 88–89; for resource procurement, 80–82; for revisiting change leadership, 92–94; for time/stress management, 83–84; views of leadership applied to, 41–50

Dean/faculty tension: over fundraising activities, 29; over role conflicts, 21–22

Deaning: Middle Management in Academe (Morris), 101

Deans: career paths over time, 10–11; conflicting demands on, 1–3; evaluation of, 104–106; innovative practices by, 45–46; lack of preparation for, 24–26; personal/professional balance by, 38–39, 82–86; profile of effective academic, 18; role conflict between institutions and, 20–22; selection of, 11–13, 95–98; socialization of, 98–100; stress suffered by, 22–24; tension between faculty and, 21–22; types of, 2–3

Deans of instruction, 3

Deanship duties: current expectations of, 15–17; difficulty of defining, 12; evolution of, 12–15; reality of today's, 17–20

Deanships: career paths to, 9–11; demographics of individuals in, 7–8; historical development of, 5; NSAD study on, 7–9; one generation ago, 6–7; reality of today's,

17–20; rethinking position of, 106–108; study on criteria for, 11–12; turn over rates for, 97–98

Department chair roles, 89–90

Department of Plant and Microbial Biology (UC Berkeley), 30

Discrimination: academic freedom free from, 68; court decisions regarding, 59–60; legal statutes prohibiting, 58–59; sexual harassment, 62–64; tenure policies and, 61–62. *See also* Minority students

Distance learning: strategies for enhancing, 70–72; using technology for, 32–33. Technology; Web courses

Diversity: dean strategies for promoting, 55–58; shifting demographics and student, 34–35; through change, 52–53. *See also* Minority students

Eastern Michigan University, 66

Education Amendments (1972), 62

Education. *See* Higher education

Emotional intelligence, 43

Equal Protection Claus, 60

Ethical behavior: of college, 86–87; promoting, 67–69

Faculty: autonomy of, 19–20; dean mediation between students and, 14; dean support of, 56–57; fundraising conflicts between dean and, 29; incongruence of system, students and, 35–38; Lake Wobegon effect and, 87; professionalization/bureaucratization of, 65–66; promoting ethical practice by, 67–69, 86–87; redefining work by, 87–88; reframing academic departments and, 88–89; response to change by, 93–94; sexual harassment by, 62–64; technology-based instruction by, 72–73; tension between deans and, 21–22; tenure policies and, 61–62. *See also* Teaching

Faculty/Chair-Related stress, 22

Fiscal resources: budgeting strategies for, 77–79; constraint challenge of, 28–30; efficient management of, 75–79; fundraising activities as, 16, 29, 80–81; impact of Bayh-Dole Act on, 81–82; procurement of, 80–82; Web course use of, 73–75

Fourteenth Amendment, 59, 60

Fundraising activities: dean/faculty conflict over, 29; fostered by deans, 16; function of, 80–81. *See also* Fiscal resources

Gender harassment, 63

Global Consortium of Higher Education (Gmelch), 95

Goldman, Sachs, and Co., 107

Harvard deanships, 5

Higher education: curricular reform and, 31–33; curricular relevance demands and, 30–31; of deans a generation ago, 7; distance learning/Web based, 32–33, 70–75; expectations by mature students of, 35–36; managing fiscal resources for, 73–82; technical advancements and delivery of, 32–34

Hiring culture, 61

Hopwood v. Texas, 60

Hostile environment, 63

Hudson Institute, 30

ASHE-ERIC
Higher Education Reports

The mission of the Educational Resources Information Center (ERIC) system is to improve American education by increasing and facilitating the use of educational research and information on practice in the activities of learning, teaching, educational decision making, and research, wherever and whenever these activities take place.

Since 1983, the ASHE-ERIC Higher Education Report series has been published in cooperation with the Association for the Study of Higher Education (ASHE). Starting in 2000, the series is published by Jossey-Bass in conjunction with the ERIC Clearinghouse on Higher Education.

Each monograph is the definitive analysis of a tough higher education problem, based on thorough research of pertinent literature and institutional experiences. Topics are identified by a national survey. Noted practitioners and scholars are then commissioned to write the reports, with experts providing critical reviews of each manuscript before publication.

Eight monographs (10 before 1985) in the ASHE-ERIC Higher Education Report series are published each year and are available on individual and subscription bases. To order, use the order form at the back of this volume.

Qualified persons interested in writing a monograph for the ASHE-ERIC Higher Education Report series are invited to submit a proposal to the National Advisory Board. As the preeminent literature review and issue analysis series in higher education, the Higher Education Reports are guaranteed wide dissemination and provide national exposure for accepted candidates.

Execution of a monograph requires at least a minimal familiarity with the ERIC database, including *Resources in Education* and the current *Index to Journals in Education*. The objective of these reports is to bridge conventional wisdom and practical research.

Advisory Board

Susan Frost
Office of Institutional Planning and Research
Emory University

Kenneth Feldman
SUNY at Stony Brook

Anna Ortiz
Michigan State University

James Fairweather
Michigan State University

Lori White
Stanford University

Esther E. Gottlieb
West Virginia University

Carol Colbeck
Pennsylvania State University

Jeni Hart
University of Arizona

Consulting Editors
and Review Panelists

Gretchen M. Bataille
University of North Carolina

Estela Bensimon
University of Southern California

Patricia Carter
University of Michigan

Esther Gottlieb
West Virginia University

Linda Johnsrud
University of Hawai'i at Mānoa

Patrick Love
Kent State University

Larry Penley
Arizona State University

Susan Twombly
University of Kansas

Recent Titles

Volume 27 ASHE-ERIC Higher Education Reports

Volume 26 ASHE-ERIC Higher Education Reports

Volume 23 ASHE-ERIC Higher Education Reports

Back Issue/Subscription Order Form

Copy or detach and send to:

Jossey-Bass, 350 Sansome Street, San Francisco CA 94104-1342

Call or fax toll free!

Phone 888-378-2537 6AM-5PM PST; Fax 800-605-2665

Individual reports:	Please send me the following reports at $24 each (Important: please include series initials and issue number, such as AEHE 27:1)

1. AEHE _____

_____

_____

$ _____ Total for individual reports

$ _____ Shipping charges (for individual reports *only;* subscriptions are exempt from shipping charges): Up to $30, add $5^{50} • $30^{01}–$50, add $6^{50} $50^{01}–$75, add $8 • $75^{01}–$100, add $10 • $100^{01}–$150, add $12 Over $150, call for shipping charge

Subscriptions   Please ❏ start my subscription to *ASHE-ERIC Higher Education Reports* for the year <u>2001</u> at the following rate (6 issues): U.S.: $108   Canada: $188   All others: $256

$ _____ Total individual reports and subscriptions (Add appropriate sales tax for your state for individual reports. No sales tax on U.S. subscriptions. Canadian residents, add GST for subscriptions and individual reports.)

❏ Payment enclosed (U.S. check or money order only)

❏ VISA, MC, AmEx, Discover Card # _____ Exp. date _____

Signature _____ Day phone _____

❏ Bill me (U.S. institutional orders only. Purchase order required.)

Purchase order #_____

Federal Tax ID 135593032   GST 89102-8052

Name _____

Address _____

_____

Phone_____ E-mail _____

For more information about Jossey-Bass, visit our Web site at:

www.josseybass.com   **PRIORITY CODE = ND1**

Mimi Wolverton is associate professor at Washington State University and current codirector of the Center for Academic Leadership. She has more than 20 years of executive experience in private sector organizations and holds a Ph.D. in leadership and policy studies from Arizona State University. Her research interests are in the areas of leadership, organizational change, educational policy, and curriculum and instructional improvement.

Walter H. Gmelch is dean of the College of Education at Iowa State University and codirector of the Center for Academic Leadership. He earned a Ph.D. in the educational executive program from the University of California–Santa Barbara. As educator, management consultant, university administrator, and former business executive, Gmelch has conducted research and published extensively on the topics of leadership, team development, conflict, and stress.

Joni Montez is a graduate student and research associate for the Center for Academic Leadership at Washington State University, working toward a Ph.D. in education with an emphasis in higher education administration. Her graduate studies focus on effective leadership and the advancement of women and minorities in the legal and educational professions.

Charles T. Nies has worked professionally in higher education for more than ten years. He holds a Ph.D. in educational administration with an emphasis on leadership from Washington State University. His areas of specialization include gender and power, multicultural education, and leadership education and development, and his research interests focus on leadership and institutional change.

LC 5215 .C35 2001 c.1
Wolverton, Mimi.
The changing nature of the
 academic deanship

DATE DUE

MAY 30 2001	
AUG 3 1 2001	

GAYLORD   PRINTED IN U.S.A.